Palgrave Advances in Luxury

Series Editors
Paurav Shukla
Southampton Business School
University of Southampton
Southampton, UK

Jaywant Singh
Kingston Business School
Kingston University
Kingston Upon Thames, UK

The field of luxury studies increasingly encompasses a variety of perspectives not just limited to marketing and brand management. In recent times, a host of novel and topical issues on luxury such as sustainability, counterfeiting, emulation and consumption trends have gained prominence which draw on the fields of entrepreneurship, sociology, psychology and operations.

Examining international trends from China, Asia, Europe, North America and the MENA region, *Palgrave Advances in Luxury* is the first series dedicated to this complex issue. Including multiple perspectives whilst being very much grounded in business, its aim is to offer an integrated picture of the management environment in which luxury operates. It explores the newer debates relating to luxury consumption such as the signals used in expressing luxury, the socially divisive nature of luxury and the socio-economic segmentation that it brings. Filling a significant gap in our knowledge of this field, the series will help readers comprehend the significant management challenges unique to this construct.

All submissions are single blind peer reviewed. For more information on our peer review process please visit our website: https://www.palgrave.com/gp/book-authors/your-career/early-career-researcher-hub/peer-review-process.

For information on how to submit a book proposal for inclusion in this series please contact Liz Barlow: liz.barlow@palgrave.com. For further information on the book proposal process please visit our website: https://www.palgrave.com/gp/book-authors/publishing-guidelines/submit-a-proposal.

More information about this series at
http://www.palgrave.com/gp/series/15396

Andrea Runfola • Matilde Milanesi
Simone Guercini

Internationalization of Luxury Fashion Firms

Examining the Business Models of SMEs

palgrave
macmillan

Andrea Runfola
Department of Economics
University of Perugia
Perugia, Italy

Simone Guercini
Department of Economics and Management
University of Florence
Florence, Italy

Matilde Milanesi
Department of Economics and Management
University of Florence
Florence, Italy

ISSN 2662-1061 ISSN 2662-107X (electronic)
Palgrave Advances in Luxury
ISBN 978-3-030-88754-4 ISBN 978-3-030-88755-1 (eBook)
https://doi.org/10.1007/978-3-030-88755-1

This Palgrave Macmillan imprint is published by the registered company Springer Nature Switzerland AG.
The registered company address is: Gewerbestrasse 11, 6330 Cham, Switzerland

To our moms, Laura, Marisa, and Silvia

Praise for *Internationalization of Luxury Fashion Firms*

"Going global is a challenge for any firm. In this volume, Runfola, Milanesi, and Guercini explore the internationalization of small- and medium-size Italian luxury fashion companies. In this specific context, the authors examine the challenges faced by smaller firms building global demand, while supporting a luxury image and managing global marketing efforts. Using a case-based approach, the authors discuss the international growth and expansion of small firms competing as style leaders in the luxury fashion goods market. This book provides valuable insights not only to students of fashion marketing and merchandising, but also to researchers in international business/marketing in general."

—Dr. Anthony Di Benedetto, Professor of Marketing and Supply Chain Management, *Temple University*, Co-Editor-in-Chief, Industrial Marketing Management

"The authors make considerable effort to reveal new insights by retracing the experience of small and medium-sized Italian luxury fashion companies, revealing an often original pathway to innovation and internationalization compared to that of the large global companies. Small and medium sized companies make a significance contribution to innovation and growth in the industry, given the importance of Italy in global luxury fashion."

—Dr. Susan Freeman, Professor of International Business, *University of South Australia*, Associate Editor, International Marketing Review

"This book brilliantly addresses the critical issues of the relationship between luxury fashion companies and the internationalization process. The authors provide in-depth knowledge and powerful insights for practitioners and academics in the global fashion industry."

—Dr. Eunju Ko, Professor of *Yonsei University*, Editor-in-Chief of Journal of Global Fashion Marketing

Contents

About the Authors

Andrea Runfola is Associate Professor of Marketing and Management in the Department of Economics at the University of Perugia, Italy. Prior to his current position, he was an Assistant Professor at the University of Perugia. He graduated in Economics and Management at the University of Florence. He then continued to pursue his Ph.D. in Marketing at the University of Urbino. Prior to joining the University of Perugia, he was a research fellow at the University of Florence, Italy. His research interests include international business, international marketing, business networks and supply chains, business models, luxury, and digitalization, with a focus, although not exclusive, on the fashion industry. He has been researching fashion and luxury for about twenty years. He is a member of the Board of the Ph.D. in Economics at the University of Perugia. He has been visiting professor at primary universities abroad. He has participated in numerous research projects. His work has been published in leading national and international journals such as *Industrial Marketing Management*, *Journal of Business Research*, *Journal of Business and Industrial Marketing*, *European Management Journal*, *International Business Review*, *Journal of Cleaner Production*, *Entrepreneurship & Regional Development*, *Journal of Global Fashion Marketing*, and *Journal of Fashion Marketing and Management*. In addition, he is the author of chapters in edited books and has written two books on the role of relationships and networks, respectively, on the internationalization of fashion retailing and technological change in business models.

Matilde Milanesi is an Assistant Professor of Marketing and Management in the Department of Economics and Management at the University of Florence, Italy. She graduated in Economics and Management at the University of Florence, where she also received her Ph.D. in Economics in 2015. She has been visiting researcher at the Centre for Science and Technology Studies, Department of Economic History, Uppsala University. She is the chief operating officer for the LabMI (Laboratory of Research in Marketing and Internationalization) at PIN, a consortium of the University of Florence. Her research interests lie in the area of international business and international marketing, industrial marketing, buyer-supplier relationships, and luxury and fashion marketing. Her works are published in academic-refereed journals such as *Journal of Business Research, Industrial Marketing and Management, International Marketing Review, Journal of Business & Industrial Marketing, Journal of Cleaner Production, Journal of International Management, and Journal of Global Fashion Marketing.* She is also the author of chapters in edited books and has published a book on liabilities and networks in the internationalization of fashion retailing.

Simone Guercini is Full Professor of Marketing and Management in the Department of Economics and Management of the University of Florence, Italy. He holds a Ph.D. in Economics at Sant'Anna School of Pisa. His research interests include business marketing, international business, qualitative research in marketing and management, and heuristics in decision-makers' behavior and cognition. He is a member of the Board of the Ph.D. in Economics at the University of Florence. He has been visiting professor at primary universities and research institutes, including the Science Policy Research Unit (SPRU), University of Sussex; Max Planck for Human Development in Berlin, Germany; Georgia State University-Center for International Business Education and Research (GSU-CIBER) at GSU and Kelley School of Business at Indiana University Bloomington, United States; and the University of Navarra, Spain. For over twenty years, he has carried out empirical research on textile and leather goods companies in Italy and has been invited to hold courses or invited to talks on the results of his research at many universities, including the Stockholm Business School, Manchester Metropolitan University, Hong Kong Polytechnic University, University of Navarra, and Grenoble School of Management. He is member of national and international academies and research groups. He has been a Ph.D. thesis evaluator for universities in Italy, United Kingdom, Switzerland, Australia, Spain, Netherlands, and India. He is senior associate editor of *Management Decision* and a member of the editorial board of other academic journals in the field of marketing and management, including *Journal of Fashion Marketing and Management*. He was associate editor of *Journal of Business Research* and *Journal of Global Fashion Marketing*. He has authored books, chapters in books and he was editor of edited books in the field of international and cross-cultural business, marketers' behavior and cognition, entrepreneurship and marketing. He has written more than eighty articles in journals including *Industrial Marketing Management*, *Global Strategy Journal*, *Journal of Business Research*, *Management Decision*, *Journal of Business and Industrial Marketing*, *European Journal of Marketing*, *International Business Review*, *International Marketing Review*, *Journal of Cleaner Production*, *Mind & Society*, *Journal of Service Theory and Practice*, *Journal of Global Fashion Marketing*, and *Journal of Fashion Marketing and Management*.

Abbreviations

B2B	business-to-business
B2C	business-to-consumer
CEO	chief executive officer
DOS	directly operated store
EBIT	earnings before interest and taxes
EBITDA	earnings before interest, taxes, depreciation, and amortization
GVC	global value chain
LOF	liability of foreignness
LON	liability of newness
LOO	liability of outsidership
LOS	liability of smallness
MNEs	multinational enterprises
SMEs	small- and medium-sized enterprises
TPOS	third-party operated store

List of Figures

1

Introduction

Why write a book on the internationalization of luxury fashion companies? Thinking of companies in this sector as international companies may seem almost obvious to many. Our personal experience quickly reminds us of traveling through airports, shopping malls, historic city centers in different countries of the world, in which we have always met the same luxury fashion brands (Gucci, Ferragamo, Chanel, Dior, Louis Vuitton, Burberry, and Valentino, to name some of the best known globally). Most of these brands are expression of luxury fashion and can be found in the vast majority of countries worldwide, with considerable visibility.

Several luxury fashion brands are an almost representative element of the globalization that has characterized the past decades. These brands are often expression of large companies, conglomerate and multinational enterprises (MNEs). The international business and international marketing literature frequently addresses these companies (Moore et al., 2010; Armitage & Roberts, 2021). However, it seems to lack a real insight into the reasons and ways in which the luxury fashion sector has become emblematic of the development of global marketers.

A. Runfola et al., *Internationalization of Luxury Fashion Firms*, Palgrave Advances in Luxury, https://doi.org/10.1007/978-3-030-88755-1_1

This book tries to address an apparent gap in the international business and international marketing literature concerning the reasons, processes, and forms assumed for the internationalization of luxury fashion companies, and the relationship between internationalization and business models.

The attention could easily fall on the most famous luxury fashion brands. In this book, however, we want to explore why luxury fashion is particularly suited to internationalization processes and has become one of the leading sectors of globalization in recent decades. In this context, the choice has been to focus on small- and medium-sized enterprises (SMEs),[1] trying to grasp the peculiar aspects supporting and characterizing their internationalization. Large companies usually have the necessary resources to establish on an international scale. However, this also happens frequently for smaller companies, making the topic worthy of further attention. On this point, the international business and entrepreneurship literature offers instead a contribution, which has been growing since at least the 1990s, as evidenced by the emphasis on born global companies (Knight & Cavusgil, 2004) and international entrepreneurship (McDougall & Oviatt, 2003). In the internationalization theory, for a long time, it appeared relatively surprising that small businesses could internationalize rapidly already in the years following their foundation. This theme has appeared strongly in literature since the 1990s in essential works on the relationship between company size and propensity to export (Bonaccorsi, 1992). However, in international luxury fashion, at least

[1] According to the European Commission (Recommendation 2003/361/EC), the category of micro and SMEs is made up of companies which employ fewer than 250 persons and have an annual turnover not exceeding 50 million euros, and/or an annual balance sheet total not exceeding 43 million euros. In particular, the book examines the Italian SMEs, which represent about 92% of the companies active in the area. Mediobanca, a leading Italian specialized financial group, together with Unioncamere, the Italian Union of Chambers of Commerce, in their annual surveys of Italian medium-sized companies, extend the parameters given by the European Commission, including in the category those companies with a turnover of no more than 355 million euros and no more than 500 employees. Regarding the fashion industry—the empirical context of this study—in addition to the dimensional parameters, it is possible to clearly distinguish between the large multinationals of luxury fashion, whether they are independent companies, such as Armani or Prada, or belonging to large global groups, such as Gucci (Kering), often with revenues well over 1 billion euros, and SMEs, of much smaller size, often independent but still operating in foreign markets.

since the Second World War, companies of this type have become widespread, so many of them could appear as "*born global ante litteram*", much anticipating a phenomenon that later became the object of attention in the literature.

One of the reasons of interest for the present study is a sectoral interpretation of the internationalization processes. Luxury fashion is a sector with particular characteristics compared to others (e.g., the food industry) in the relationship between industry and distribution, resulting in luxury fashion companies that are often vertically integrated. This element favors a particular form of internationalization linked to the opening of retail stores abroad. Recently, the relationship between industry and distribution has also been characterized by the technological change taking place, particularly on the distribution side, with the development of e-commerce and a new types of marketing activities connected to this phenomenon (Guercini et al., 2018).

In this book, however, the focus is not on the internationalization of distribution and retail activities. Instead, it is on luxury fashion companies with a manufacturing base, although they may also have invested in distribution with direct and, often, exclusive channels as part of the vertical integration strategies (Runfola & Guercini, 2013).

The attention for the internationalization of luxury fashion companies, therefore, is on the internationalization of SMEs for which there may be various liabilities (smallness and often newness) in addition to those typical of internationalization processes, such as foreignness and, increasingly, outsidership (Johanson & Vahlne, 2009). Luxury fashion is also a context in which companies operate in a consumer market and with a network of suppliers, business customers, and influencers.

In this study, the field of research, in the empirical investigation, is even better defined, focusing on companies that have a manufacturing base and are located in a specific country, Italy, which has long played and is still playing a significant and recognized role in the global luxury fashion industry. The international success of Italian luxury fashion companies has often been identified concerning specific characteristics, such as a demanding internal consumption, a peculiar distribution system, and a decisive role of manufacturing in sectors such as textiles, clothing, and leather goods (Porter, 2011); a solid propensity to share external resources within local production systems (Becattini, 1990); a significant presence in the highest and most exclusive segments of luxury fashion (Guercini & Milanesi, 2017).

However, which is the current global scenario of luxury fashion?

Here, it is enough to recall some aspects of the luxury world that the book will explore. The concept of luxury in fashion has undergone an evolution over time, as in other luxury sectors (such as food or furniture). From a concept of elite luxury for a segment of the super-rich and affluent consumers, through processes of democratization, it has expanded its sphere of influence to include new segments (Kapferer & Bastien, 2012). Luxury now ranges from a extreme luxury (Guercini & Milanesi, 2017) to affordable luxury (Cabigiosu, 2020). The product categories associated with luxury have also evolved. In the shoe-making industry, for example, luxury comprises handmade leather shoes as well as sneakers. The evolution of the concept and the product categories of luxury over time, therefore, have made it possible for both upper- and middle-class segments (Guercini & Runfola, 2016) to have the opportunity to approach luxury fashion goods.

This process is enriched today by the fundamental importance of the new generations as consumers of luxury. Millennials and Generation Z are the new targets of luxury. These generations are bearers of new values and new demand, such as sustainability issues (Bakir et al., 2020). Keywords such as circular economy, second-hand, and fair trade principles are becoming more and more critical for fashion players (Todeschini et al., 2017). New generations also search for experiences that combine the digital and physical dimensions. For example, digitalization has heavily affected the customer journey of luxury customers (Guercini et al., 2020). According to the True-luxury Global Consumer Insight (2021) from BCG-Altagamma,[2] luxury for the new generations should evolve toward "clienteling 2.0" that requires attention to customer relations, personalization of experiences in digital and offline channels, and the use of new technologies. The impact of the COVID-19 pandemic has reinforced these aspects. In addition, the issue of how to rethink the younger

[2] https://web-assets.bcg.com/f2/f1/002816bc4aca91276243c72ee57d/bcgxaltagamma-true-luxury-global-consumer-insight-2021.pdf

generations' luxury experience according to new approaches has emerged recently. For example, the luxury sector has paid attention to the theme of gamification (Batat, 2019) as part of a general trend toward virtualization of the experience (Jung et al., 2019), considered by BCG-Altagamma as one of the most promising areas of evolution. Large luxury players, such as Gucci, have committed to developing their solutions and partnerships with gaming companies.[3] The world of luxury is, therefore, a world in constant evolution from the perspective of the dynamics of consumption.

There are also global trends on the side of the international marketing strategies of luxury companies. Undoubtedly, the promotion of initiatives linked to sustainability appears to be an evident trend. Luxury companies are increasingly paying attention to environmental and social sustainability in their business. This attention translates into multiple activities, such as the reorganization of production processes to improve efficiency and reduce the environmental impact, the use of sustainable materials, and the waste management (Hennigs et al., 2013; Karaosman et al., 2020). Also, the growing attention in marketing communications to social issues linked to the enhancement of differences, inclusiveness, the absence of any kind of discrimination. Concerning the need to build sustainable supply chains and exploit the "Made in", another phenomenon that can be observed especially in luxury fashion is the reshoring (Fratocchi et al., 2014; Młody & Stępień, 2020), which "refers to a generic change of manufacturing location with respect to a previous off-shore location" (Młody & Stępień, 2020, p. 143), and the back-reshoring, which is particularly relevant for luxury companies and refers to "a transfer of manufacturing activities back to the company's home country" (Młody & Stępień, 2020, p. 143).

Moreover, the luxury industry presents peculiarities regarding different countries. Alongside traditional primary luxury markets, such as the US and Japan, China has acquired crucial importance for many luxury companies for over a decade now, especially for players in the fashion industry. The luxury market has been enriched over time by new markets that

[3] https://www.pambianconews.com/2020/05/28/febbre-videogame-gucci-si-allea-con-tennis-clash-294401/

have flanked the traditional luxury destinations. Bain & Company (2020) identifies the period of China's explosion in luxury, at the beginning of the last decade, as the "Chinese shopping frenzy" to point out the expansion of luxury consumption in the Chinese market and the attempt by large luxury companies to target this market.[4] However, the most important international markets for luxury players, other than some European markets (such as Germany, France, UK, and Spain) include Russia, United Arab Emirates, and South Korea (Guercini et al., 2020). As it is well known, one asset that luxury companies exploit is the "Made in" effect. Made in Italy, made in France, or made in the US, to cite a few, are essential in the value proposition of different luxury players to develop internationally. However, a specific "Made in" (such as the Made in Italy) may have different potentials and perceptions (e.g., the value perceived, luxury categories associated) among foreign markets.

Luxury fashion, within the broader world of luxury, is a protagonist of all these trends. Luxury fashion is one of the main areas of personal luxury goods. According to Bain & Company (2020), in 2019, before the COVID-19 pandemic, personal luxury goods reached 281 billion euros out of a total of the luxury sectors that amounted to 1.268 billion euros.[5] It was the second luxury sector for sales, after luxury cars. In this scenario, the COVID-19 pandemic has influenced the market. The 2020 Luxury Goods Worldwide Market Study[6] by Bain & Company outlines that the overall luxury market, which encompasses both luxury goods and experiences, shrank by 20% to 22%, reaching approximately one trillion euros globally, back to 2015 levels. Regarding the experiences (including luxury hospitality, cruises, and fine dining), they were heavily impacted (−56%), and their recovery will be slow since they depend on tourist flows. Experience-based goods (including fine art, luxury cars, private jets and yachts, fine wines and spirits, and gourmet food) were less impacted, declining by only 10%, and the recovery will be faster due to positive consumption dynamics. The market for personal luxury goods, which is the "core of the core" of luxury segments and includes luxury fashion

[4] https://www.bain.com/insights/eight-themes-that-are-rewriting-the-future-of-luxury-goods/
[5] https://www.bain.com/insights/eight-themes-that-are-rewriting-the-future-of-luxury-goods/
[6] https://www.bain.com/insights/the-future-of-luxury-bouncing-back-from-covid-19/

goods, contracted for the first time since the continuous growth started in 2009, falling by 23% to hit 217 billion euros. More in general, the luxury industry is now dominated by uncertainty caused by uncertain course of the pandemic in many areas.

Regarding these trends and data and, more in general, the luxury industry, works by scholars and practitioners have always addressed large companies' strategies. How luxury SMEs internationalize and relate to these (and other) global trends is substantially unexplored. Concerning this issue, the book is aimed at providing a deeper understanding regarding luxury fashion SMEs, as fashion is considered one of the most prolific domains in terms of internationalization. In other words, the gap that this book wants to fill concerns the internationalization of luxury fashion SMEs. These companies are often as international as the larger and multinational ones. However, due to their size, they set specific business models to operate in the global luxury industry. Luxury fashion SMEs deal with an uncertain world, matching the company's characteristics with the luxury industry's evolutionary trends. While business models of large luxury players, especially the fashion ones, have received significant attention, there is a lack of studies on SMEs' business models. Hence, the book intends to show the main features of the business model of luxury fashion SMEs and to what extent the business model dimensions relate to internationalization. More specifically, the focus is on manufacturing luxury fashion SMEs. To this aim, the book addresses three research questions, as shown in Fig. 1.1: *(a) Why do luxury fashion SMEs internationalize?, (b) How do luxury fashion SMEs set the internationalization process?, and (c) What are the implications of internationalization for the business models of luxury fashion SMEs?* The book will discuss these three questions and provide the main components of the business model of luxury fashion SMEs.

Hence, the structure of the book is the following.

Chapter 2 discusses the relationship between luxury and internationalization. In particular, the main features of luxury companies are outlined and the motives that lead them to face internationalization processes, often since their establishment. Among these, some relevant motives are discussed: the size of the demand, global image, luxury customers' profiles, and the management of distribution and communication channels.

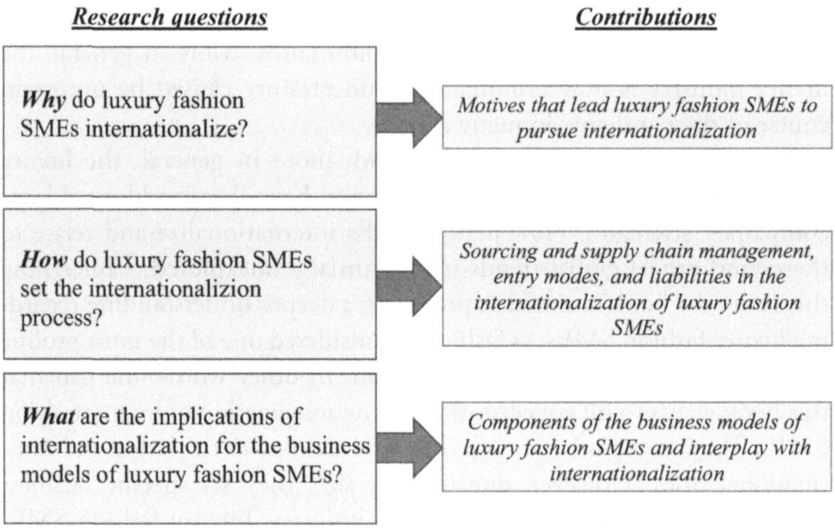

Fig. 1.1 The research questions of the book. (Source: Authors' elaboration)

Luxury fashion companies may find insufficient demand in the country of origin to guarantee their development. In other words, the demand in the domestic market can be limited, especially for niche or elitist products, and this can push luxury fashion companies to turn to foreign markets to find broader demand. In recent years, there has been a strong growth of luxury demand, motivated both by the expansion of the number and profiles of customers interested in purchasing luxury brand products (a phenomenon linked to the democratization of luxury) and the increasing number of customers from emerging countries.

Additionally, a global image of luxury brands is essential for obtaining legitimacy and orienting customers' preferences. A global image is connected to the affirmation of a global reputation. Moreover, it relates even more to global recognition, which has long been indicated among the elements that characterize the brand strategy of companies in the luxury industry. There is also the need for luxury fashion companies to associate the brand with contexts that can confirm the desired image of the luxury product, such as those cities that are commonly connected to the sale of luxury products, for example, Paris, Milan, London, New York, and

Monte Carlo. Another factor that pushes the internationalization of luxury fashion companies, even SMEs, is represented by the characteristics of the customers of luxury products, namely their cosmopolitan character, attention to the international scenario, frequent travels to various destinations for business and leisure reasons. Lastly, the need to manage distribution and communication channels, including the physical and the digital ones, have pushed luxury companies to select the areas in which to invest through the opening of retail stores and invest in digital platforms. The management of distribution and communication channels is related to different types of advantages: the economy of scope (distribution formats and merchandising models can be replicated on a large scale and for different brands); the economy of scale in the purchase or rental of physical spaces and advertising spaces (both in the traditional and digital media). These benefits can be maximized on an international scale.

While Chap. 2 tries to answer why luxury companies undertake internationalization paths, Chap. 3 analyzes how such companies internationalize. The chapter examines the internationalization of luxury fashion companies in terms of entry and expansion into foreign markets. The chapter proposes an overview of the literature on the internationalization process of luxury fashion companies. It is highlighted that while contributions to brand management in international markets are many, research on the internationalization of luxury fashion companies has not yet reached a level of maturity and depth. Besides the internationalization of management of know-how, the two main and most evident dimensions of the internationalization of fashion companies are the sourcing of products from foreign markets and the operation of retail stores by international fashion retailers. Thus, the chapter addresses a specific dimension of the internationalization of luxury fashion companies, namely the management of the retailing phase through the opening of retail stores in foreign markets, which represents the most evident aspect of the internationalization of luxury fashion companies. The efforts of luxury fashion companies in the retail side are one relevant aspect of the international growth, alongside other marketing efforts related to brand positioning and communication. However, luxury fashion companies' supply chain and sourcing strategies play an essential role in configuring the luxury offer. Supply chain management is critical to compete in local and international markets and ensure product delivery whose characteristics should match customer requirements. The opening of retail stores and the supply chain management and sourcing strategies are not the only ways luxury fashion companies have to approach foreign markets. E-commerce is increasingly related to the internationalization of luxury fashion companies. The use of an e-commerce platform (the company's digital store or the selling of luxury fashion products through online multi-brand retailers) transcends international boundaries and enables consumers from almost all over the world to get in touch with a company. The chapter concludes with an analysis of the main difficulties that luxury fashion companies may find in their internationalization process, namely the liability of foreignness and outsidership, and how such liabilities may turn into assets.

Chapter 4 shows the relationships between internationalization and the business models of luxury fashion players. It aims to understand how internationalization represents one of the main components of the business models of luxury fashion companies and explains the different interpretations of business models within the literature, presenting the most recent academic debate. Moreover, starting from the need to consider various business models in the luxury industry that emerge from the empirical world, the chapter proposes a potential business model taxonomy, with four types of business models related to different actors in the luxury industry: (a) large luxury fashion MNEs; (b) independent entrepreneurial SMEs; (c) vertically integrated luxury suppliers; (d) digital native luxury brands. The large luxury fashion MNEs business model includes companies with a global scale presence, both in production and selling markets. These companies manage well-known brands at an global level. Within this macro-typology, it is possible to include large conglomerate companies (such as LVMH, Kering, Richemont), and MNEs with established brands, such as global players from France (e.g., Chanel or Hermès), Italy (e.g., Prada, D&G, and Armani), the US (e.g., Ralph Lauren or Michael Kors), and the UK (e.g., Burberry and Stella McCartney). The second business model is that of independent firms with an entrepreneurial nature and small-medium size. Within this typology, the entrepreneur plays an important role. Such companies base much of their international success on the ability of the entrepreneur to develop strategies on how to approach foreign markets and meet customer requirements. Within this business model, family is often a relevant asset to develop in international markets. Similarly, the country of origin and the ability to conciliate smallness with foreign expansion play a relevant role. A third business model is that of vertically integrated suppliers. The luxury fashion industry offers possibilities in terms of integration along the supply chain. Suppliers may follow the road of proposing their collections, even though they originate from the upper stages of the pipeline. For example, yarn or fabric producers may start apparel production in the textile-clothing supply chain and set up a new brand to relate with final consumers. Their business model is characterized by high manufacturing competencies that can be exploited internationally and the availability to experiment with new ways to compete in international markets. Lastly, the fourth business model combines digital dimensions with manufacturing skills. This typology includes business models that emerge from the advent of digital innovation and new technologies and refers to new entrepreneurial initiatives, often linked to start-ups in the digital environment.

Chapter 5 introduces the methodology adopted in the book, that of case study, followed by the empirical context of this study, namely the Italian luxury fashion industry. The chapter then presents two cases of artisan companies in local clusters: Sapaf and Bontoni. Sapaf is a historic company in the Florentine territory (Tuscany region) that produces luxury bags, both for third parties and with its brand. Bontoni is from the Montegranaro district (Marche region), and it is a handcrafted shoemaker that creates and produces luxury men's shoes. The two companies share their belonging to the leather goods sector and are both presented as emblematic cases of small-sized luxury fashion companies located in industrial districts with a strong vocation for internationalization since their origins.

Chapter 6 presents four Italian luxury medium-sized companies that have undertaken dimensional growth and international expansion: Fabiana Filippi, Antonelli Firenze, Monnalisa, and E.Marinella. Fabiana Filippi is a womenswear total look brand with a vocation for cashmere knitwear. Based in Umbria, it creates, produces, and distributes Made in Italy collections according to sustainability practices, positioned in the contemporary luxury segment. Antonelli Firenze is a Tuscan brand founded in 1950 that offers a total look defined as “by women for women”, whose stylistic vision is constantly looking for natural elegance, without excesses and Italian imprint. Monnalisa is another Tuscan brand founded in Arezzo in 1968 that designs, produces, and distributes luxury childrenswear, constantly focusing on innovation, digitalization, and opening of retail stores in foreign markets. Finally, E.Marinella is a historical sartorial company founded in Naples in 1914. It is an international icon for luxury ties production within the menswear luxury fashion. Some of the most influential world personalities wore E.Marinella’s ties contributing to the company’s worldwide awareness.

Chapter 7 discusses the six cases starting from the theoretical background proposed in Chaps. 2, 3, and 4. More specifically, the motives for internationalization, features of the internationalization process and entry modes, and the business models are outlined by considering the main findings emerging from the six cases. Next, the chapter answers the three questions mentioned earlier. Then, by jointly considering theoretical insights and empirical findings, it proposes arguments to explain why luxury fashion SMEs are international, how they internationalize, and the implications of internationalization for their business models. Finally, the chapter proposes the business model of luxury fashion manufacturing SMEs, its components, and the relationship between them and the internationalization process. The chapter emphasizes the manufacturing nature of the companies that drives and influences the internationalization process, and also compares the emerging business models of luxury SMEs with large global players in the luxury industry to point out differences and similarities.

Chapter 8 concludes the book by addressing the main theoretical and managerial implications emerging from the research. Theoretically, it discusses the contribution in terms of response to the research gaps of the literature by highlighting the “genetic” nature of internationalization of luxury SMEs and the role of the liability of localness. Finally, from a managerial point of view, the concluding section proposes some practical implications for entrepreneurs, managers, and those who are interested in the luxury business. The managerial implications can be applied to luxury SMEs in general, not only those in the fashion industry. Entrepreneurs and managers of luxury SMEs should avoid the liability of localness, consider internationalization as transversal to the business model, embrace the global trends of luxury, balance growth in foreign markets with the economic and financial sustainability of the company, take into due consideration how to benchmark with other luxury companies (MNEs and SMEs). These implications represent food for thought for luxury fashion players and, in general, for those who are interested in high-end or luxury products.

References

Armitage, J., & Roberts, J. (2021). The globalisation of luxury fashion: The case of Gucci. *Luxury, 6*(3), 227–246.

Bain & Company. (2020). *Eight themes that are rewriting the future of luxury goods*. Available at: https://www.bain.com/insights/eight-themes-that-are-rewriting-the-future-of-luxury-goods/

Bakir, A., Gentina, E., & de Araújo Gil, L. (2020). What shapes adolescents' attitudes toward luxury brands? The role of self-worth, self-construal, gender and national culture. *Journal of Retailing and Consumer Services, 57*, 102208.

Batat, W. (2019). *Digital luxury: Transforming brands and consumer experiences*. Sage.

Becattini, G. (1990). The Marshallian industrial districts as a socio-economic notion. In F. Pyke (Ed.), *Industrial districts and inter-firm co-operation in Italy* (pp. 37–51). International Institute for Labour Studies.

Bonaccorsi, A. (1992). On the Relationship Between Firm Size and Export Intensity. *Journal of International Business Studies, 23*(4), 605–635.

Cabigiosu, A. (2020). An overview of the luxury fashion industry. In *Digitalization in the luxury fashion industry. Palgrave advances in luxury*. Palgrave Macmillan.

Fratocchi, L., Di Mauro, C., Barbieri, P., Nassimbeni, G., & Zanoni, A. (2014). When manufacturing moves back: Concepts and questions. *Journal of Purchasing and Supply Management, 20*(1), 54–59.

Guercini, S., & Milanesi, M. (2017). Extreme luxury fashion: Business model and internationalization process. *International Marketing Review, 34*(3), 403–424.

Guercini, S., & Runfola, A. (2016). How western marketers respond to the new middle class in emerging market cities: The case of Italian fashion marketers. *International Business Review, 25*(3), 691–702.

Guercini, S., Bernal, P. M., & Prentice, C. (2018). New marketing in fashion e-commerce. *Journal of Global Fashion Marketing, 9*(1), 1–8.
Guercini, S., Ranfagni, S., & Runfola, A. (2020). E-commerce internationalization for top luxury fashion brands: Some emerging strategic issues. *Journal of Management Development, 39*(4), 423–436.
Hennigs, N., Wiedmann, K. P., Klarmann, C., & Behrens, S. (2013). Sustainability as part of the luxury essence: Delivering value through social and environmental excellence. *Journal of Corporate Citizenship, 52*, 25–35.
Johanson, J., & Vahlne, J. E. (2009). The Uppsala internationalization process model revisited: From liability of foreignness to liability of outsidership. *Journal of International Business Studies, 40*(9), 1411–1431.
Jung, J., Yu, J., Seo, Y., & Ko, E. (2019). Consumer experiences of virtual reality: Insights from VR luxury brand fashion shows. *Journal of Business Research, 130*, 517–524.
Kapferer, J. N., & Bastien, V. (2012). *The luxury strategy: Break the rules of marketing to build luxury brands*. Kogan Page Publishers.
Karaosman, H., Perry, P., Brun, A., & Morales-Alonso, G. (2020). Behind the runway: Extending sustainability in luxury fashion supply chains. *Journal of Business Research, 117*, 652–663.
Knight, G., & Cavusgil, S. T. (2004). Innovation, organizational capabilities and the born-global firm. *Journal of International Business Studies, 35*(2), 124–141.
McDougall, P. P., & Oviatt, B. M. (2003). Some fundamental issues in international entrepreneurship. *Entrepreneurship Theory & Practice, 18*(27), 1–27.
Młody, M., & Stępień, B. (2020). Principles of reshoring development in luxury goods sector. *International Journal of Management and Economics, 56*(2), 140–158.
Moore, C. M., Doherty, A. M., & Doyle, S. A. (2010). Flagship stores as a market entry method: The perspective of luxury fashion retailing. *European Journal of Marketing, 44*(1/2), 139–161.
Porter, M. E. (2011). *Competitive advantage of nations: Creating and sustaining superior performance*. Simon and Schuster.
Runfola, A., & Guercini, S. (2013). Fast fashion companies coping with internationalization: Driving the change or changing the model? *Journal of Fashion Marketing and Management, 17*(2), 190–205.
Todeschini, B. V., Cortimiglia, M. N., Callegaro-de-Menezes, D., & Ghezzi, A. (2017). Innovative and sustainable business models in the fashion industry: Entrepreneurial drivers, opportunities, and challenges. *Business Horizons, 60*(6), 759–770.

2

Luxury and Internationalization: Motives and Features

2.1 Motives for the Internationalization of Luxury Companies

This chapter examines the motives for internationalization that are specific to luxury companies. The existence of reasons, antecedents, or specific conditions, which can push luxury companies toward internationalization, is a topic that has only recently been the subject of attention (Bai et al., 2021). Recent literature has noted that internationalization characterizes a typical business model of extreme luxury fashion companies. Therefore, internationalization is a constitutive element of a specific business model rather than a strategy for a business model already defined (Guercini & Milanesi, 2017). Recently, scholars have argued that the business model can play a role in generating early internationalization, such as that characterizing the so-called born globals (Hennart et al., 2021). More specifically, Hennart et al. (2021) argue that an important reason for the rapid international expansion of some SMEs has to do with their business model. Some SMEs have a business model that facilitates rapid foreign sales growth, primarily SMEs characterized by a niche business model, whose products and services do not require

A. Runfola et al., *Internationalization of Luxury Fashion Firms*, Palgrave Advances in Luxury, https://doi.org/10.1007/978-3-030-88755-1_2

host country-specific marketing mix adaptations and do not need foreign-based after-sales services.

In this chapter, we examine the existence of factors that push luxury fashion companies to internationalize, which derive from their specific characteristics and the context in which they operate. Thus, these factors act as motives for internationalization. In the present chapter, we present these factors as hypotheses formulated starting from the characteristics of companies and the luxury sector.

Most of the research on luxury takes the perspective of demand and, in particular, consumption processes (Tynan et al., 2010; Cristini et al., 2017; Thomsen et al., 2020), leaving in the background the corporate actors processes and their motivations (Kapferer, 2014). However, the condition of luxury business can affect the formation of the company's identity and, therefore, affects the opinions and choices of the corporate actors, also concerning internationalization. Regarding luxury fashion companies, very famous brands immediately come to mind that are well-known not only in their country of origin but at an international and often global level (Cooper, 2012). Many of these brands are known to consumers in the main international markets and, in several cases—such as Gucci, Prada, Louis Vuitton—their fame does not seem to know boundaries. Thus, many luxury fashion brands are known globally, and their international development has had a significant boost over the last few decades (Fernie et al., 1997; Jin & Cedrola, 2016). This notoriety is linked to various factors, such as the visibility in traditional and new media, both in the form of advertising and editorial content, the evident presence in almost all cities of developed countries and metropolises around the world, and even in cities not necessarily of the first or second tier of newly developed countries, starting with China (Zhang & Kim, 2013).

If we take some of the most famous and important luxury fashion brands, also in terms of size, such as Luis Vuitton, Gucci, or Hermès, although being different from each other in terms of brand identity, they have in common notoriety and prestige that is undoubtedly at an international or global level. This element partly affects the globalization process that has characterized the markets in past decades, which has assumed particular intensity in the nineties of the last century and at the beginning of the new century (Kapferer & Bastien, 2012). Globalization is taking place hand in hand with the transformation of luxury during the last half-century. From “a niche research domain” (Kapferer & Bastien, 2012, p. 473) to one of the world’s largest industries in terms of size and international diffusion, so much so that it is addressed as “abundant rarity”, recalling how a traditional feature of luxury today reveals almost paradoxical traits (Kapferer, 2012). The luxury sector includes companies and brands globally recognized; this has been particularly true in recent decades and may depend on contingent factors. In our opinion, however, alongside factors of a more contingent nature, there are other more persistent elements, which find their *raison d’etre* in the specificity of the market, industry, and organizations engaged in this sector. In this chapter, however, we will focus, above all, on recognizable reasons, as they are predominantly non-contingent and linked to the nature of the market and luxury companies, which make internationalization of particular importance. Indeed, we can recognize various reasons that push luxury companies, especially the fashion ones, to seek international development, even when they are not large companies in size.

In the following sections of this chapter, we present possible motives that specifically push the internationalization of luxury fashion companies. Among these, some relevant motives include the size of the demand, since luxury companies seek foreign markets to obtain additional volumes of sales; the global image, essential for obtaining legitimacy and orienting consumer preferences; the characteristics of luxury customers, such as international mobility and specificity of lifestyle; the management of distribution and communication channels, including physical and digital channels. These motives, representing a non-exhaustive classification, are shown in Fig. 2.1 and discussed in the following sections.

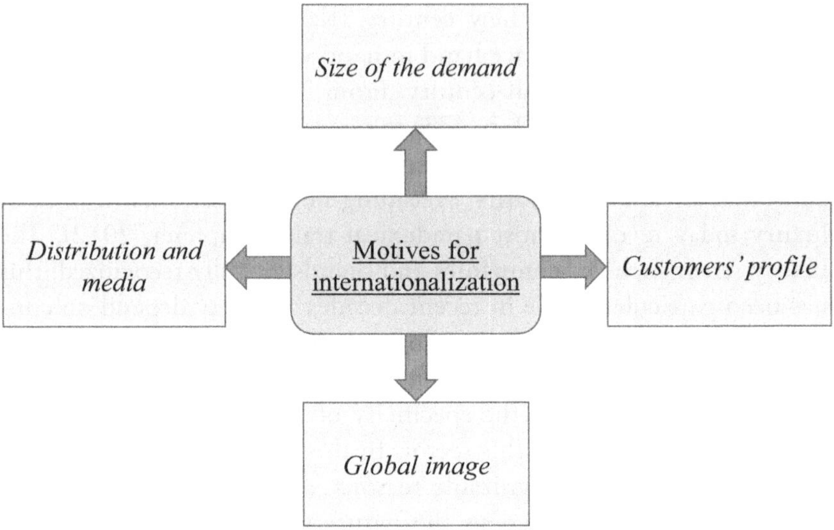

Fig. 2.1 Motives for luxury fashion firms' internationalization. (Source: Authors' elaboration)

2.2 The Size of the Demand

The dimensional scale of the potential or actual demand for luxury fashion products in the country of origin can represent a reason for the company to cross national borders and internationalize. Due to the elitist nature of the products they offer, designed for a specific segment, luxury fashion companies may find insufficient demand in the country of origin to guarantee their development, also considering the offer proposed by competitors. Thus, the demand in the domestic market can be limited, especially for niche or elitist products, which can push companies to turn to foreign markets to find broader demand.

This issue is not only true for large luxury fashion companies with a national base in small countries, which may find in their country of origin a low demand (an example is the production of luxury fashion goods by the Swiss Richmond compared to the Swiss market for the same category of products). Instead, it may also regard small companies based in relatively large countries (e.g., small artisan producers of Italian leather goods and luxury accessories) when the demand in the domestic market is relatively small, and there are many competitors. In these cases, when the foreign demand is broader, the international development is an opportunity to seize, also through indirect export.

There has been a strong growth of luxury demand in the last years, motivated both by the expansion of the number of buyers interested in purchasing luxury brand products (democratization of luxury), and the arrival of substantial numbers of buyers from new markets (buyers from emerging countries) (Quach & Thaichon, 2017). In the last decades, many consumers, traditionally excluded from the luxury market, expressed a growing desire to acquire luxury items, enforcing the idea that everyone has a "right" to access the luxury market (Granot et al., 2013). However, this does not mean that national demand becomes sufficient. Furthermore, the increasing number of buyers from emerging countries relates to a push toward internationalization (Guercini & Runfola, 2016).

The growth in demand for luxury products, therefore, increases and drives the search for foreign markets. In parallel with the growth in demand, academic research on luxury has grown too. The growth of luxury is, therefore, also an object of interest for scholars: from a niche area "attracting mainly historians, philosophers, moralists, sociologists, and economists, luxury has become a prolific research theme in equally as many managerial domains, including marketing, finance, human resources, sustainable development, strategy, supply chains, and law" (Kapferer, 2016, p. 473).

The luxury product has characteristics that orient it, by definition, to a relatively smaller demand, or at least it was initially so. The growth of the luxury market has been substantial in the last three decades and characterized by a progressive concentration of the leading players, evidenced by the fact that in 2019 the top ten global luxury players exceeded half of the total turnover of the first hundred players (Deloitte, 2020). The demand for luxury goods has constantly been growing in the quarter of a century preceding the COVID-19 pandemic (BCG & Altagamma, 2019). This growth process has led the luxury market to take on enormous dimensions. In the textile-clothing sector, the turnover of the luxury market has had a sustained trend over the last few decades: in 2019, the leading hundred global luxury players, among which textile-clothing represents the first component, have had an annual growth of turnover of over 5% (Deloitte, 2020).

This development corresponds to an increase in the overall global volumes of demand. The size of global demand is enormous today and makes luxury one of the major global industries. Moreover, even more important, the production of luxury goods is relatively concentrated in few developed countries, while the demand is increasingly distributed in new countries. According to the data of Deloitte, one of the countries in which production is concentrated, Italy, has 22 of the top 100 global companies with 12% of the production of the top 100 luxury companies, against a gross domestic product of around 2% of the world: it is clear that companies in this country, on average smaller than the sector average, must address a demand outside their national borders.

The growth in demand for luxury goods refers to the so-called democratization and the development of accessories and licenses. This phenomenon has seen consistent growth in the number of people interested in luxury goods, even among those who would not fit into traditional luxury buyer profiles (Dubois & Laurent, 1996). We will give more attention to this type of profile, often interested in accessories or cheaper luxury products, in the section of this chapter dedicated to customers' profiles as a motive for internationalization. Democratization means that, alongside the iconic products with a high unit price (clothing, bags, watches, jewelry, up to luxury cars and yachts), accessible only to a part of customers with high purchasing power, many lower-priced products, especially accessories (belts, wallets, eyeglasses, scarfs, etc.) are added to the collections, still marked by the luxury brand. The issue of democratization is characterized, for example, by an evolution of demand and its segmentation, as well as by a strong orientation toward the growth of luxury companies. In other words, the democratization of luxury not only has a presupposition on the demand side but corresponds to a growth of companies oriented toward offering licensed accessories and products (perfumes, eyewear) with relatively much more accessible prices (Silverstein & Fiske, 2003). An emblematic example of this is the spread, starting from the 1980s, of companies such as Cartier or Cardin, which started to disseminate and "accessorize" their brands, making them accessible to a much wider public than their traditional "élite" clientele. This phenomenon generated in many cases a spectacular growth of the turnover of these firms. For example, Luis Vuitton in 1977 was a family business with sales under $20 million. Twenty years later, its turnover exceeded 1 billion and was the base for creating the LVMH group (Guercini, 2017).

Ultimately, demand has grown significantly since the mid-1990s for at least two significant reasons, which have been previously mentioned: on the one hand, the extension, from the upper class to the middle class, of customers potentially interested in luxury products (Aldrich, 1989); on the other hand, the arrival of large numbers of customers from emerging countries, who joined those in advanced countries. These two lines of demand expansion did not come alone, but they also emerged thanks to companies' policies that repositioned many fashion brands in the luxury segment (Guercini & Runfola, 2016). Figure 2.2 represents the growth dynamics for the demand for luxury goods based on democratization and globalization.

The growth of the luxury market in single countries is not a sufficient motivation for internationalization: if the individual markets grow, this is not a factor of internationalization in itself, because the home market could also be growing, giving a space for business development without the efforts required by internationalization. Today's reality tells us another story: the luxury offers are attributable to

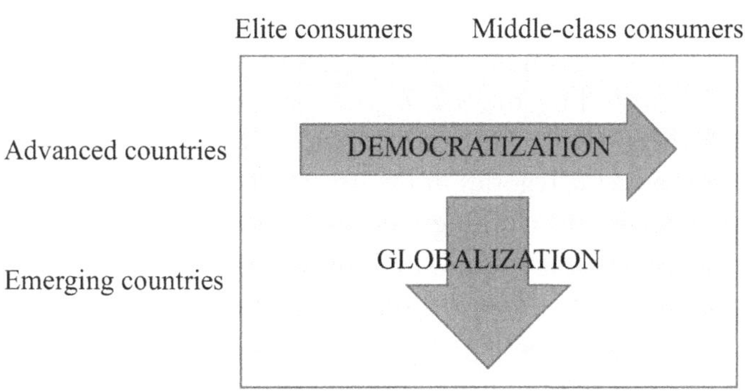

Fig. 2.2 The dynamics of growth in the demand for luxury goods. (Source: Authors' elaboration)

"ubiquitous brands". The global development of brands has been traced back to the presence of local demand with characteristics that are partly present transversally between the different countries (cross-border segments), and only in part specific and exclusive to the local context. Looking for a cross-border luxury market segment can push to standardization, diversifying the locations but adopting a global approach for luxury brands (Liu et al., 2016).

However, the size of the market must be assessed not on the overall demand for a specific country but on a more specific basis, that is, at least at the level of single luxury product categories. In the various categories of goods, luxury represents a component generally characterized by a higher unit value but with a numerical one, understood as the number of buyers and units sold, which is more limited than the premium segment or the average mass market.

Thus, expanding the geographical horizon means looking for a broader demand base, which may not be enough if luxury fashion companies remain local. This is especially true when the product targets specific segments such as market niches. Even luxury fashion SMEs can find in internationalization a potential demand adequate to the needs of their development.

The size of the demand as a motive for the internationalization of luxury fashion companies depends on the product category. Following Berry (1994), practically all product categories can include a luxury version. From this perspective, it is possible to identify different classifications. A recurring classification used in corporate documents is the one that distinguishes between fashion, fashion accessories, perfumes and cosmetics, hard luxury, including the *art de la table*, superyachts, and a residual category "others" (Bellaiche et al., 2010). Another classification includes four main product categories in luxury, which are: (1) fashion, intended mainly as textiles and clothing (couture, ready-to-wear) but also accessories, such as leather goods; (2) perfumes and cosmetics, which concerns both companies specialized in production and licensees; (3) wines and spirits; (4) watches and jewelry (Jackson, 2004). To these categories, however, we can undoubtedly add others: (5) luxury cars; (6) luxury hotels and tourism services; (7) catering and luxury food; (8) luxury boats, such as superyachts and pleasure boating in general. In addition to physical products, there are luxury services that complement physical products or are autonomous (Le & Quy, 2020).

2.3 The Global Image

The global image is a feature that luxury fashion companies can seek as an element of legitimacy toward customers looking for a product with characteristics of excellence globally recognized. Global image and internationalization can represent a marketing objective of luxury fashion companies regardless of size, as it is not an expression of large volumes but legitimacy toward an elite target. When having a global image represents a legitimizing factor toward customers, be they in the country of origin of the company or other countries, the search for a global image for the company, the brand, and products are sought after. Global reputation is included among the critical elements associated with luxury brands (Fionda & Moore, 2009) and helps motivate the purchase, together with other elements, such as the heritage and history of the brand artisanship (Liu et al., 2016).

The affirmation of a "global reputation" (Nueno & Quelch, 1998; Okonkwo, 2007) and, even more, of a "global recognition" (Fionda & Moore, 2009) has long been indicated among the elements that characterize the brand strategy of companies in the luxury industry. In particular, Nueno and Quelch (1998) recognized that the international scope is a fundamental feature of luxury brands, indicating the global reputation as a characteristic shared by traditional luxury brands, which enjoy worldwide notoriety (Nueno & Quelch, 1998). As already mentioned, luxury companies can be characterized by a business model that supports a path to early internationalization, as was recently highlighted for born globals (Hennart et al., 2021). The relationship between luxury fashion and internationalization seems to have specific characteristics compared to luxury in other sectors (e.g., food and wine). Even in the past, luxury fashion stores were in the most prestigious international locations (such as New York, Tokyo, London, Milan, and Monte Carlo.).

There is also the need to associate the brand with contexts that can confirm the desired image of the luxury product. For example, it is usual to highlight the role of the cities. They are often international capitals of luxury, in which retail stores sell the brand. These cities include major fashion capitals (e.g., New York, London, Milan, Paris) or minor centers but strongly connected to luxury consumption (e.g., Monte Carlo, Porto Cervo, Forte dei Marmi, Portofino, Saint Tropez). It is not just a question of indicating where the luxury products are sold but also demonstrating the brand's international presence, as evidenced by very long lists of places that often appear on websites, store windows, or shopping bags. In other words, luxury fashion companies want to highlight their internationality as a feature that strengthens the brand's legitimacy even in the domestic market.

The presence in multiple geographical contexts can have a relapse in terms of the image of the luxury fashion brand, assuming more significant importance than other factors. In particular, we can hypothesize that the luxury fashion brand with only a local presence could appear less significant and legitimate in the eyes of the actual or potential customer. To cope with this position of weakness, the company may have to incur costs for other activities to give prestige to the brand. By addressing these additional costs, we can imagine that the lack of internationalization produces a "liability of localness" for the brand with a lack of international image, as shown in Fig. 2.3.

Fig. 2.3 Global luxury fashion image: is there liability of localness? (Source: Authors' elaboration)

An improper development of a global image for the luxury fashion brand can lead to risks, such as the one deriving from over-localization. Over-localization occurs where the activities in a foreign market can inadvertently overly indulge the customer, leading to confusion about the brand's identity and the country of origin (Liu et al., 2019). This phenomenon relates to the choice between standardization and localization, in which over-localization is a negative consequence of excessive localization. In this sense, a certain degree of standardization corresponds to maintaining the same image across different countries and, therefore, a greater connection with worldwide brand identity.

An example of localization that can lead to over-localization is the rebranding intended as a local language translation of the brand, particularly relevant in China, where companies from various sectors have translated their brand into Chinese ideograms as a way to use ideograms with a positive value. Many companies have carefully avoided these more pronounced forms of rebranding in the luxury sector, fearing that this could generate a form of over-localization. While brands like Coca-Cola or Carrefour have proceeded to translate their name into Chinese ideograms, luxury fashion brands like Armani or Ermenegildo Zegna have carefully avoided forms of adaptation that involve excessive localization, keeping the same brand both in the country of origin and globally. Other brands, such as Pirelli, have proceeded, at least initially, to the translation. Then, they have returned to the formulation of the brand in the alphabet adopted in the country of origin, parallel with the company's progressive positioning in the luxury segment (Guercini & Ranfagni, 2013).

2.4 The Characteristics of Luxury Customers

A factor that pushes the internationalization of luxury fashion companies, even SMEs, is represented by the characteristics of the customers of luxury products, namely their cosmopolitan character, attention to the international scenario, frequent travels to various destinations for business and leisure reasons. These are recurring characteristics in consumer research, particularly from market segmentation research, in which these characteristics correspond to the profiles of the luxury segments that emerge strongly from segmentation processes (BCG & Altagamma, 2019).

Given the characteristics of the customer of luxury fashion products in terms of exposure to the international context, luxury fashion companies must "follow" the customer worldwide, not to leave space for competition or lose potential customers. Literature noted that the global customer of luxury products has cosmopolitan traits, being extensively exposed to other cultures (Loureiro & de Araújo, 2014). Such exposure, enhanced by global media, gives rise to entrepreneurs and managers with international profiles (e.g., Italian nationality, with the headquarters of their company in the United Arab Emirates, a residence in Spain, and a frequent presence for work reasons in Ireland or the United States). Although the crisis caused by the COVID-19 pandemic has put mass tourism at risk, it may not have greatly limited the movements of these elites. Even without referring to an extremely elitist consumer, who is very frequently exposed to other cultural contexts, in recent times the majority of consumers has come in contact with the offer of other countries, at least regarding the main global markets for distribution and consumption of luxury. These luxury consumers, so exposed to an international context, develop a more international perception of themselves, less oriented to the local context (Cleveland et al., 2011; Riefler et al., 2012). The development of this profile naturally tends to meet an equally international distribution of luxury products (Kapferer, 2014), which, due to its elitist tendency, does not necessarily correspond to large retail chains, known to the general public and as such visible and object of aspiration by less than elitist and, consequently, larger groups of potential customers.

The international and cosmopolitan characters of such consumers do not mean that the traits of the national culture of their country of origin are lacking: there are specific traits of the Russian elite luxury consumer, distinguishable from those of the Chinese elite luxury consumer (Liu et al., 2019). Accordingly, alongside the great attention paid by marketing research to the country of origin effect concerning the offer (products, brands, designers, companies, etc.), the same reasoning can be done concerning consumers from different countries: a specific country of origin of the offer can take on different meanings and image depending on the cultural traits of the target consumer (Pucci et al., 2017).

As for demand characteristics, these have evolved in parallel with the democratization of luxury (Dubois & Laurent, 1996). From the nineties, a third type of luxury consumer has emerged, defined as "excursionist". This is because, in contrast to the "excluded", who have no access to luxury goods, and to the "affluent", whose access is more or less permanent, their purchase and consumption of luxury items are occasional. Excursionists buy and consume luxury goods only in specific circumstances. They buy and consume luxury items as an exceptional moment, sharply contrasting with their daily lifestyle. The excursionists are strongly different from the "haves", which consume luxury as an expression of their *art de vivre*. Behavior varies between different people depending on their susceptibility to interpersonal influence. To describe consumer behavior of luxury brands, scholars consider some interpersonal aspects such as the following: snobbery; conspicuousness; hedonism; perfectionism; other economic, societal, political factors. Value relates to beliefs that guide the selection or evaluation of desirable behavior (Schultz & Zelezny, 1999), including displaying status, success, distinction; the human desire to impress others; the nature of financial, functional, and individual utilities. It is possible to recognize four latent dimensions which adds luxury value in the consumer's perception (Wiedmann et al., 2009, p. 629):

1. Financial dimension of luxury value, including aspects such as price, resale cost, discount, investment, the value of the product expressed in dollars, euros, yen, as well as what is given up or sacrificed to obtain it.
2. Functional dimension of luxury value, including basic utilities such as quality, uniqueness, usability, reliability, and durability.
3. Individual dimension of luxury value, including customers' orientation toward luxury consumption and personal aspects such as materialism.
4. Social dimension of luxury value, including perceived utility individuals acquire with products or services recognized within their social group(s), such as conspicuousness and prestige, to cite a few.

In the past, the luxury market was segmented in a straightforward manner. As a result, two broad clusters were identified (Dubois & Laurent 1996): (1) the "excluded", who had no access to this market, including the vast majority of the population; (2) the "affluent", namely consumers who, whether "old money" or "nouveaux riches", had both the desire and the financial ability to make luxury their *art de vivre*.

The distinction between different customer segments concerned the "wealth" and "need for status" parameters, distinguishing four different customer profiles (Han et al., 2010). These profiles have no national connotations and can be read as transversal to different countries, even if the categorization responds to a recognizable society, especially in a given era (nineteenth–twentieth century) and in the context of Western countries. The first, the "patrician", is among those who have high levels of wealth and do not have a high need for status, so the customers' goal is to leave signals through the possession of luxury goods, but only to other patricians, for whom the need for status is relatively low. Instead, those who have a higher need for status fall into the category of the "upstart", or "new money", strongly oriented to be dissociated from those who have no wealth. Among those who do not have wealth, the "proletarians" are distinguished from the "poseurs", the former are not engaged in any signal, not having many possibilities, and not being motivated by a strong need for status. In contrast, despite not having the financial means, the latter aspires to achieve status and, therefore, imitate the new money as much as possible (Han et al., 2010, p. 17). Those most interested in status aspects may also be interested in purchasing recognizable branded products in different contexts for these segments.

A much more articulated segmentation is proposed in recent years by BCG and Altagamma. It considers both the factors that define the profiles and the analysis of the adopted behaviors. Table 2.1 lists the customer segments.

2.5 Distribution and Communication Channels

The internationalization of luxury fashion companies also relates to the evolution of distribution and communication. Regarding distribution, the last decades have witnessed a process of vertical integration by luxury fashion companies. Vertical integration means that luxury companies

Table 2.1 An example of cross-country segmentation of the luxury market

Segment	Buyers' characteristics and consistency of the segment	Favorite categories	Main country—segment % in each country
Absolute luxurer	"Luxury as a commodity" 2.3 million consumers Total spend €73 billions Mainly aged 35–45, 55% female European élite, classy, and elegant Exclusivity, customization, connoisseur, known brands	Jewelry Watches Clothing Vacation	United Kingdom (15%), Italy (14%), United States (13%), Germany (11%)
Megacitier	"World is my city, the city is my world" 2.9 million consumers Total expenditure €52 billions Mainly aged 25–35, 55% female Part of global élite, shop a lot when abroad Quality, customization, latest trends	Leather Goods Clothing Jewelry Vacation	Brazil (23%) China (21%) Russia (14%) South Korea (12%)
Experiencer	"Luxury is real only when shared" 2.9 million consumers Total expenditure €37 billions Mainly aged 40–50, 60% male Looking for a unique experience, discrete style, superior customer care	Vacation Food & wine Sophisticated experiences	Germany (19%) France (16%) United Kingdom (15%) United States (14%)
Fashionista	"In fashion I trust" 2.9 million consumers Total expenditure €24 billions Mainly aged 35–40, 60% female Cool, sexy and exclusive, unique details, trend-setter, highly opinionated, knows everything	Handbags Clothing Shoes New designers	United States (13%) China (13%) UK, Italy, and Russia (12% each)

(continued)

Table 2.1 (continued)

Segment	Buyers' characteristics and consistency of the segment	Favorite categories	Main country—segment % in each country
Social wearer	"Luxury should drive a better world" 2.3 million consumers Total expenditure €24 billions Mainly aged 35–40, 55% female Social responsibility, sustainability, and innovation Emotional connection with brands	"made in" Handbags Clothing Food & wine	Brazil (15%) United States (12%) Italy (11%) Germany (8%)
Little prince	"Luxury is my fun" 1.8 million consumers Total expenditure €18 billions Mainly aged 18–25, 55% male Looking for innovation and being cool Impulsive shoppers, brands over quality, adorned aesthetic	Clothing Leather goods Cosmetics	South Korea (12%) Brazil (9%) Russia (8%) Germany (7%)
Status seeker	"I show that I exist" 2 million consumers Total expenditure €14 billions Mainly aged 35–40, 55% male Search for external approval Followers, brand visibility to show off	Bags Shoes Clothing Well-known brands	Russia (11%) South Korea (11%) United Kingdom (9%) United States (8%)
Classpirational	"I saw it on my boss" 3.1 million consumers Total expenditure €9 billions Mainly aged 30–40, 60% male Looking for timeless and trusted brands Follower and unsophisticated luxury consumer, value for money	Clothing Perfumes Cosmetics Bags	South Korea (20%) Russia (15%) Italy (13%) Japan (12%)

Source: Authors' elaboration from BCG & Altagamma, 2016

have set, in a decisive way since the nineties, development strategies of their direct distribution, with investments in the opening of retail stores worldwide (Guercini & Runfola, 2016). This development of direct distribution channels has not only affected the luxury sector as a whole but has been particularly evident in the field of luxury fashion. In other words, to develop distribution, companies have tried to select the areas in which to invest, and these have been the large metropolises and the main cities or shopping centers in many foreign countries.

Distribution and communication represent the competitive advantage of the luxury conglomerates developed globally over the last few decades. Some of these (such as LVMH, Kering, or Essilor-Luxottica) have reached such dimensions that they are among the most influential corporate groups in the world. The direct control of distribution channels is related to different types of advantages: the economy of scope (distribution formats and merchandising models can be replicated on a large scale and for different brands); the economy of scale in the purchase or rental of physical spaces (stores in the city center, in urban or suburban shopping malls, including many factory outlet centers) and advertising spaces (both in the traditional and digital media). These advantages can be of considerable size for luxury conglomerates because they operate on many markets or in the global luxury market generally considered. The achievement of these advantages connected to a large scale of reproduction of distribution and communication models, or the purchase of large volumes of physical and advertising spaces, reaches high levels in the internationalization of luxury fashion companies. In other words, even for companies based on significant markets (e.g., United States and China), it would be difficult to fully exploit these advantages if national borders were not crossed.

Analyzing the role of distribution and communication for luxury fashion companies means considering the different environments in which these activities take place today, which include:

1. the physical environment, that of the retail stores in which the luxury fashion brands carry out both communication and sales activities; it is a context that, for decades, has catalyzed a significant part of the investments of luxury fashion brands, with notable effects both on the financial assets and the real estate market, especially in the central areas of major or more attractive and prestigious urban centers;

2. the traditional media, including the printed media (the magazines of the sector, particularly well-known and relevant in the fashion and luxury sector, such as *Vogue*), television and radio, which can be less incisive for communication of luxury fashion brands but are manned (especially television) by some of the companies in the sector;
3. the digital environment is acquiring increasing relevance, in which there are different types of distribution channels (direct, indirect, single-brand, multi-brand, etc.) and different types of communication spaces (the company website, social media, search engines, blogs, etc.).

Physical distribution for luxury fashion companies has been massively characterized by internationalization through the opening of retail stores abroad, a phenomenon whose importance for companies in the sector is testified by the impact of investments in the opening of new retail stores out of total corporate investments (Guercini & Runfola, 2015a, 2016, 2019). The international character of this distribution is also signaled by the centrality of some specific places in which to set up stores, which correspond to luxury and fashion streets in the center of cities of greater dimension, attractiveness, and prestige. Fashion and luxury streets of cities such as Paris, London, or Milan ensure a basin of attraction beyond the national borders of France, the United Kingdom, or Italy, respectively. The prestigious location of luxury fashion retail stores justifies the prices for the acquisition, leasing, and commercial start-up estimated by specialized operators, such as Cushman and Wakefield (2019), for the real estate industry that estimates the cost per square meter or square yard.

In the case of online distribution and luxury fashion e-commerce, there are groups of companies specialized in multi-brand distribution (e.g., Yoox, Farfetch, Luisa Via Roma) that have achieved success thanks to their strong international appeal, to the point that, for some of them, the digital stores are replicated in many languages. In addition, they hire native speakers from different countries to guarantee accurate customer service. The latter is a fascinating element to indicate these companies' international dimensions (Guercini & Runfola, 2015b).

Being oriented toward a global clientele, luxury fashion companies look for global partners, both media and influencers, for their communication activities. Influencers take on particular relevance and visibility in the luxury fashion sector: Chiara Ferragni and Mariano Di Vaio from Italy, to cite a few, are well-known worldwide and often collaborate with global luxury fashion brands for their digital campaigns. Concerning the more traditional media, the case of Condé Nast, a company that publishes *Vogue* magazine and other relevant fashion magazines, highlights the existence of global communication partners. Even if this is not the only case, its visibility and notoriety make it an emblematic case; as is well known, *Vogue* magazine has various editions published in various national markets. Thus, *Vogue* magazine remains very relevant and influential despite the growing importance of communication activities on digital media (especially Instagram that is the leading social media for the digital campaigns of luxury fashion brands).

2.6 Motives and Features: Some Conclusions

If it is easy to observe a progressive internationalization over the last decades of both companies, the competitive context, and the luxury fashion market, the literature on this topic is not as mature. Only a few authors have examined the characteristics and motives for the internationalization of companies in this specific sector. In this chapter, we have proposed a systematization that seeks to answer the question about the specific features and motives for the internationalization of luxury fashion companies, and contributes to the international marketing and international business literature. Even though this literature does not address the topic directly and systematically, it still offers various practical elements to approach it.

The motives for the internationalization of luxury fashion companies identified in the previous pages emerge from the joint consideration of the literature and empirical research conducted by the authors of this book in the past two decades. Such motives are now fully represented in Fig. 2.4. The specific motives we have examined do not represent an exhaustive picture, but they can provide the first basis to discuss and guide future research. While the focus of this chapter has been the motives for internationalization (*why?*) of luxury fashion companies, the

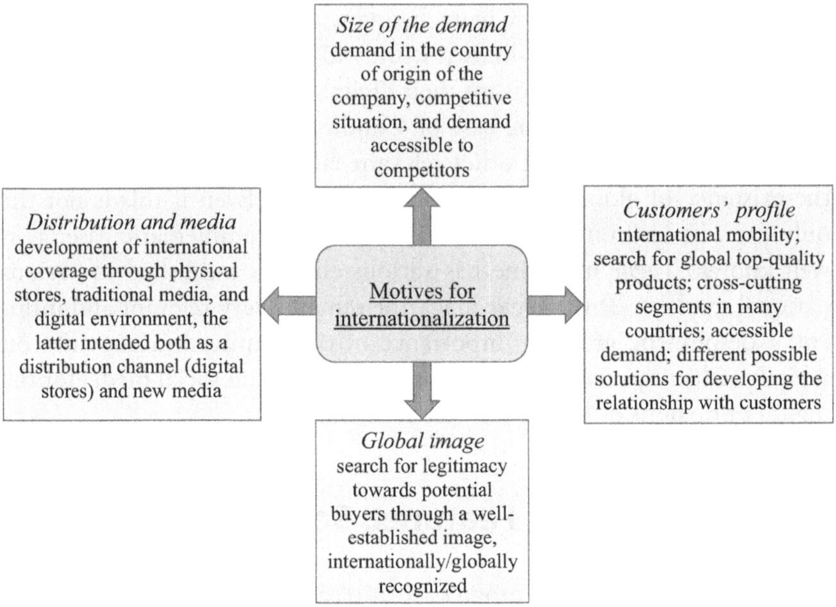

Fig. 2.4 Motives for internationalization: an analysis. (Source: Authors' elaboration)

following two chapters outline how luxury fashion companies internationalize (the features of their internationalization process and the entry modes), and what are the business models of luxury fashion companies and the link between the business model and internationalization.

References

Aldrich, N. W. (1989). *Old money: The mythology of America's upper class*. Vintage.

Bai, H., He, W., Shi, J., McColl, J., & Moore, C. (2021). Internationalization strategies of emerging market multinationals in luxury fashion retailing—Case study of Shandong Ruyi Group. *Thunderbird International Business Review, 63*(3), 319–327.

BCG & Altagamma (2016). The true luxury global consumer segmentation, available at https://www.youtube.com/watch?v=Jp1ARkFWBrE

BCG, & Altagamma. (2019). *2019 True-luxury global consumer insight*. Available at: http://media-publications.bcg.com/france/TrueLuxury%20Global%20Consumer%20Insight%202019%20-%20Plenary%20-%20vMedia.pdf

Bellaiche, J. M., Mei-Pochtler, A., & Hanisch, D. (2010). The new world of luxury. Caught between growing momentum and lasting change. .

Berry, C. J. (1994). *The idea of luxury: A conceptual and historical investigation* (Vol. 30). Cambridge University Press.

Cleveland, M., Papadopoulos, N., & Laroche, M. (2011). Identity, demographics, and consumer behaviors: International market segmentation across product categories. *International Marketing Review, 28*(3), 244–266.

Cooper, N. (2012). Emerging luxury strategies: Insights from BrandZ. *Hermes, 19*, 61.

Cristini, H., Kauppinen-Räisänen, H., Barthod-Prothade, M., & Woodside, A. (2017). Toward a general theory of luxury: Advancing from workbench definitions and theoretical transformations. *Journal of Business Research, 70*, 101–107.

Cushman & Wakefield. (2019). *Main streets across the world*. Available at https://www.cushmanwakefield.com/en/singapore/insights/main-streets-across-the-world-2019

Deloitte. (2020). *Global power of luxury goods 2020. The new age of fashion and luxury*. Available at https://www2.deloitte.com/it/it/pages/consumer-business/articles/deloitte-global-powers-of-luxury-goods-2020%2D%2D-deloitte-italy%2D%2D-c.html

Dubois, B., & Laurent, G. (1996). The functions of luxury: A situational approach to excursionism. *ACR North American Advances, 23*, 470–477.

Fernie, J., Moore, C., Lawrie, A., & Hallsworth, A. (1997). The internationalization of the high fashion brand: The case of central London. *Journal of Product & Brand Management, 6*(3), 151–162.

Fionda, A. M., & Moore, C. M. (2009). The anatomy of the luxury fashion brand. *Journal of Brand Management, 16*(5), 347–363.

Granot, E., Russell, L. T. M., & Brashear-Alejandro, T. G. (2013). Populence: Exploring luxury for the masses. *Journal of Marketing Theory and Practice, 21*(1), 31–44.

Guercini, S. (2017, March). *Principles of luxury and managing luxury brands*, lecture notes, Grenoble Graduate School of Business.

Guercini, S., & Milanesi, M. (2017). Extreme luxury fashion: Business model and internationalization process. *International Marketing Review, 34*(3), 403–424.

Guercini, S., & Ranfagni, S. (2013). Integrating country-of-origin image and brand image in corporate rebranding: The case of China. *Marketing Intelligence & Planning, 31*(5), 508–521.

Guercini, S., & Runfola, A. (2015a). Internationalization through e-commerce. The case of multibrand luxury retailers in the fashion industry. In *International marketing in the fast changing world*. Emerald Group Publishing Limited.

Guercini, S., & Runfola, A. (2015b). Small-medium sized manufacturers' internationalization through retail store openings abroad: A study of the Italian fashion industry. In *International marketing in the fast changing world*. Emerald Group Publishing Limited.

Guercini, S., & Runfola, A. (2016). How western marketers respond to the new middle class in emerging market cities: The case of Italian fashion marketers. *International Business Review, 25*(3), 691–702.

Guercini, S., & Runfola, A. (2019). Developing fashion retail operations to growth in emerging markets. *Journal of Global Fashion Marketing, 10*(2), 145–162.

Han, Y. J., Nunes, J. C., & Drèze, X. (2010). Signaling status with luxury goods: The role of brand prominence. *Journal of Marketing, 74*(4), 15–30.

Hennart, J. F., Majocchi, A., & Hagen, B. (2021). What's so special about born globals, their entrepreneurs or their business model? *Journal of International Business Studies*, 1–30.

Jackson, T. (2004). A contemporary analysis of global luxury brands. *International Retail Marketing, 1*, 155–169.

Jin, B., & Cedrola, E. (2016). Overview of fashion brand internationalization: Theories and trends. In *Fashion brand internationalization* (pp. 1–30). Palgrave Pivot.

Kapferer, J. N. (2012). Abundant rarity: The key to luxury growth. *Business Horizons, 55*(5), 453–462.

Kapferer, J. N. (2014). The artification of luxury: From artisans to artists. *Business Horizons, 57*(3), 371–380.

Kapferer, J. N. (2016). The challenges of luxury branding. In *The Routledge companion to contemporary brand* (pp. 505–523). Routledge.

Kapferer, J. N., & Bastien, V. (2012). *The luxury strategy: Break the rules of marketing to build luxury brands*. Kogan Page Publishers.

Le, N. T. C., & Quy, V. T. (2020). Personal values of luxury services consumption: A Confucian culture perspective. *Journal of International Consumer Marketing, 32*(4), 300–312.

Liu, S., Perry, P., Moore, C., & Warnaby, G. (2016). The standardization-localization dilemma of brand communications for luxury fashion retailers' internationalization into China. *Journal of Business Research, 69*(1), 357–364.
Liu, S., Perry, P., & Gadzinski, G. (2019). The implications of digital marketing on WeChat for luxury fashion brands in China. *Journal of Brand Management, 26*(4), 395–409.
Loureiro, S. M. C., & de Araújo, C. M. B. (2014). Luxury values and experience as drivers for consumers to recommend and pay more. *Journal of Retailing and Consumer Services, 21*(3), 394–400.
Nueno, J. L., & Quelch, J. A. (1998). The mass marketing of luxury. *Business Horizons, 41*(6), 61–61.
Okonkwo, U. (2007). What's in a name? The history of luxury fashion branding. In *Luxury fashion branding* (pp. 13–58). Palgrave Macmillan.
Pucci, T., Casprini, E., Guercini, S., & Zanni, L. (2017). One country, multiple country-related effects: An international comparative analysis among emerging countries on Italian fashion products. *Journal of Global Fashion Marketing, 8*(2), 98–112.
Quach, S., & Thaichon, P. (2017). From connoisseur luxury to mass luxury: Value co-creation and co-destruction in the online environment. *Journal of Business Research, 81*, 163–172.
Riefler, P., Diamantopoulos, A., & Siguaw, J. A. (2012). Cosmopolitan consumers as a target group for segmentation. *Journal of International Business Studies, 43*(3), 285–305.
Schultz, P. W., & Zelezny, L. (1999). Values as predictors of environmental attitudes: Evidence for consistency across 14 countries. *Journal of Environmental Psychology, 19*(3), 255–265.
Silverstein, M. J., & Fiske, N. (2003). Luxury for the masses. *Harvard Business Review, 81*(4), 48–59.
Thomsen, T. U., Holmqvist, J., von Wallpach, S., Hemetsberger, A., & Belk, R. W. (2020). Conceptualizing unconventional luxury. *Journal of Business Research, 116*, 441–445.
Tynan, C., McKechnie, S., & Chhuon, C. (2010). Co-creating value for luxury brands. *Journal of Business Research, 63*(11), 1156–1163.
Wiedmann, K. P., Hennigs, N., & Siebels, A. (2009). Value-based segmentation of luxury consumption behavior. *Psychology & Marketing, 26*(7), 625–651.
Zhang, B., & Kim, J. H. (2013). Luxury fashion consumption in China: Factors affecting attitude and purchase intent. *Journal of Retailing and Consumer Services, 20*(1), 68–79.

3

The Internationalization of Luxury Fashion

3.1 The Internationalization of Luxury Fashion Companies: An Overview

Luxury fashion brands are among the most recognized consumer brands worldwide, mainly consumed for the emotional and passionate feelings they provoke (Kapferer & Tabatoni, 2011). Accordingly, quality, reputation, and brand image—as shown in the previous chapter—are critical features for attracting clients and justifying high prices. Besides the primary role of the brand, luxury fashion companies are increasingly characterized by another feature, namely their international, or even global, scope. In the last decades, luxury fashion companies have surfed the waves of globalization and put internationalization at the center of their marketing strategy. The turbulent global competitive environment of the last two decades, recently aggravated further by the COVID-19 pandemic, has heavily influenced the repositioning and redesign of luxury goods and pushed luxury companies toward innovation and diversification to reach new targets. Alleres (2003) present three categories of luxury, namely accessible luxury, middle luxury, and inaccessible luxury, the latter characterized by the presence of "extreme luxury fashion

A. Runfola et al., *Internationalization of Luxury Fashion Firms*, Palgrave Advances in Luxury, https://doi.org/10.1007/978-3-030-88755-1_3

companies" (Guercini & Milanesi, 2017). More in general, the recent literature on the luxury landscape has pointed out how the current global scenario proposes new challenges for luxury companies that call for a rethinking of their marketing strategies (Chandon et al., 2016). New opportunities for luxury companies arise from consumers in emerging markets (Cavusgil & Buckley, 2016; Guercini & Runfola, 2019) and new digital technologies, especially the role of digital marketing tools and e-commerce (Moore & Doyle, 2010; Kapferer & Bastien, 2012; Chandon et al., 2016; Guercini & Runfola, 2016; Mir-Bernal et al., 2018).

Concerning luxury fashion companies, some phenomena appear as particularly relevant, such as the global spread of luxury fashion stores both in mature and emerging countries; the shift from independent, family-owned small companies to multinationals (such as LVMH, Kering, and Richemont), as a consequence of M&A strategies; the building of global value chains; a "democratization" of luxury, with the launch of accessory and makeup lines with affordable prices and the consequent rise of the so-called accessible luxury; the growth of emerging markets that account for over half of worldwide luxury goods sales (Moore et al., 2000; Vickers & Renand, 2003; Shukla, 2012; Guercini & Milanesi, 2017). Additionally, the designer's role in luxury fashion companies can gain iconic status and increase the international prestige of such companies. The design signature of Versace, Ralph Lauren, Tommy Hilfiger, Giorgio Armani, to cite a few, can "override the importance of other qualities, such as country of origin. Their design signature permeates into other related activities, such as perfume and cosmetics, interiors and household products, hotels, restaurants and so on" (Bruce & Kratz, 2007, p. 137). Luxury fashion brand owners, such as Gucci and LVMH, contend internationally renowned fashion designers (Marc Jacobs for LVMH, Riccardo Tisci for Givenchy and Burberry, Tom Ford and Alessandro Michele for Gucci are just a few examples) to provide a creative direction of the *maison* and reinforce their international image related to the fact that designers often become international celebrities.

Thus, studying how luxury fashion companies expand in foreign markets is intriguing and worthy of further investigation. Contributions on brand management in international marketing are not new (Moore, 1998; Okonkwo, 2016; Fionda & Moore, 2009). In their international development, luxury fashion brands can assume the characteristics of a global brand, namely a worldwide standardized brand image, a wide international presence (foreign markets served), a perception by consumers regarding the global availability of the brand (Craig & Douglas, 2000). To reach the status of global luxury fashion brand, the standardization of brand communication is required (Moore et al., 2000), as well as a balance between product and branding strategies (Wigley et al., 2005), which may require some adaptation to local consumers, especially in the context of emerging markets (Liu et al., 2016). However, while contributions on brand management in international markets are many, research on the internationalization of luxury fashion companies has not yet reached a level of maturity and depth.

Moore and Burt (2007) suggest that besides the internationalization of management of know-how, the two main and most evident dimensions of the internationalization of fashion companies are the sourcing of products from foreign markets and the operation of retail shops by fashion retailers within foreign markets. A stream of recent literature addresses a specific dimension of the internationalization of luxury fashion companies, namely the management of the retailing phase through the opening of retail stores in foreign markets (Guercini & Runfola, 2015a; Milanesi, 2020). The opening of retail stores is the most evident aspect of the internationalization of luxury fashion companies (Moore & Burt, 2007). The investment by luxury fashion companies in the retailing stage has become one of the main international marketing strategies to enter foreign markets (Guercini & Runfola, 2016). Moore, Doherty, and Doyle (2010) maintain that the opening of stores abroad, especially flagship stores, represents the essential market entry mode for luxury fashion companies. In other words, the internationalization of luxury fashion companies concerns, among other strategies, the managing of retail stores in foreign markets and the definition of an appropriate retail store mix to rely on for international development (Guercini & Milanesi, 2016).

Along with the stores opening abroad, scholars discuss the role of new digital technologies and the Internet as facilitators of the international expansion of luxury fashion companies (Guercini & Runfola, 2015b; Chandon et al., 2016). Berridge (2018) observed that a considerable challenge for luxury fashion is represented by digitalization, as many luxury fashion companies have been reluctant to keep up with the digital age. An emblematic example is Chanel, still resistant to the digitalization of its brand and against the opening of an e-commerce platform. The main reason for this reluctance is the fear of not providing the same luxury experience as in bricks and mortar, with possible negative consequences for the brand reputation, which is a critical asset for the success of a luxury brand. In other words, the main concern of luxury fashion brands is that online sales, especially through third-party marketplace platforms, may cheapen the brand and reduce its exclusivity. Even when resistance to online is reduced, and a luxury fashion brand decides to sell through its e-commerce platform, there is the problem of adequately structuring one's digital presence to replicate an exclusive experience comparable to that provided in physical stores. The creation of experiences is an impelling issue and a relevant factor of success for all companies, especially when such experiences must be translated in an online world, in a proper shopping atmosphere (Hansen & Jensen, 2009; Dion & Arnould, 2011). This is particularly true for luxury companies, as they have to keep a high level of exclusivity, reputation, and identity in the online world (Rovai, 2018). However, it seems that in recent years, luxury fashion brands have accepted the digital challenge by managing their online presence through their website, their e-commerce platform, the sale of their products on third-party e-commerce platforms, and the presence on social media (Cabigiosu, 2020). In particular, the possibility to deliver an interactive and satisfying Internet experience has given rise to the wide use of social media, even in the case of luxury fashion companies (Kim & Ko, 2012; Dauriz et al., 2014; Godey et al., 2016; Romão et al., 2019), with an increasing role of fashion blogging and fashion influencers as new ways to communicate the brand (Kulmala et al., 2013; Jin et al., 2021). Furthermore, it has been discussed that e-commerce could represent a means for incrementing the sales of luxury fashion companies in foreign markets, also thanks to the development of luxury multi-brand online retailers (Mir-Bernal et al., 2018; Guercini et al., 2020a). Thus, the digitalization of luxury fashion companies, in particular through the development and management of an e-commerce platform, represents an effective international marketing strategy to reach new targets, namely the new generations of young luxury consumers, such as Generation Z

(Bakir et al., 2020), and new markets (Guercini & Runfola, 2015b; Chandon et al., 2016).

Another evident dimension of the internationalization of fashion companies is the sourcing of products from foreign markets (Moore & Burt, 2007). Concerning luxury fashion companies, two issues appear relevant: sourcing raw materials and semi-finished products and outsourcing production phases to suppliers in domestic and foreign markets. About the latter, there are real clusters of luxury in which first-, second-, or even third-tier suppliers are a vital part of the supply chain of luxury fashion brands (Caniato et al., 2011). An example is provided by the luxury district in Tuscany, Italy, in which there is a constellation of SMEs located in the various production phases that are part of the supply network of global luxury fashion companies, such as Gucci, Balenciaga, YSL, as first-, second- or third-tier suppliers, characterized by craftsmanship, experience, production skills, and tradition (Milanesi et al., 2020).

What is interesting to notice is that the internationalization of luxury fashion companies involves different types of players. The most evident players are the leading global griffes, such as Chanel, Prada, Gucci, YSL, and Salvatore Ferragamo. Although there are no doubts about the leading role of such large companies, the luxury arena is dotted with SMEs and family-owned luxury fashion brands, which have received less academic contributions. These companies, albeit small in size, have a high international reputation and presence. The Italian luxury fashion is full of examples of SMEs and family businesses (Corbetta et al., 2015) with a strong international vocation. Runfola, Ranfagni, and Guercini (2018) examine the case of a luxury fashion family business, Missoni, to explain how it develops a strong international brand through a complex system of brand values, the family dimension as a company-unifying force in the internationalization process, the integration of distribution channels and strategic parallelism between branding and building consumer relationships in international markets.

Starting from this background, the chapter, in the next sections, examines the internationalization of luxury fashion companies focusing mainly on three dimensions: the opening of stores in foreign markets, sourcing strategies, and e-commerce, as shown in Fig. 3.1. For each, the chapter examines the traits that characterize luxury fashion companies, the type

Fig. 3.1 Main internationalization dimensions of luxury fashion companies. (Source: Authors' elaboration)

of companies involved in the process, the strengths and difficulties encountered in their internationalization path.

3.2 The Opening of Stores in Foreign Markets

Much attention has been devoted to the internationalization of fashion firms (e.g., Fernie et al., 1997; Hines & Bruce, 2007; Guercini & Runfola, 2010; Tavoletti, 2011; Jin & Cedrola, 2016). Fashion companies are consistently recognized as the most prolific of international players, especially in the retail environment (Wigley & Moore, 2007), and they operate in a dynamic, fast-evolving context characterized by growing complexity and fierce competition (Newman & Cullen, 2002). As observed by Castelli and Brun (2010, p. 24), "the dramatic shift in scale and power of major retail chains in the market, the advent of own brands retail networks, the nature of sourcing and supply chain (SC) decisions which are increasingly global in nature, are just some of the issues that have contributed to this complexity". In this scenario, further aggravated in the last year by the COVID-19 pandemic, the failure or success of fashion companies largely depend on the organizations' flexibility and responsiveness (Christopher et al., 2004). Thus, a significant aspect of the internationalization of fashion firms is the process of stores opening as an entry mode strategy in foreign markets. The theme of store opening is central to a large and growing number of firms in the fashion industry, including luxury fashion brands as leading global players. Recent studies have stressed the role of direct distribution channels to enter new markets and overcome commercial intermediaries (Guercini & Milanesi, 2016, 2019).

Since the late 1990s, the owners of luxury fashion brands began to rapidly develop their distribution channels by opening retail outlets, extending the control over the supply chain, from manufacture and design to retailing (Fionda & Moore, 2009). For example, luxury fashion brand Louis Vuitton has heavily invested in the opening of stores (from 800 in 1998 to 1500 five years later) (Jackson, 2004), and some luxury fashion companies, such as Gucci, have begun to buy back franchises to ensure a significant level of control over their brand (Moore & Birtwistle, 2005). The rationale behind this strategic choice is to secure control over the whole customer experience, including the personal assistant in stores, and keep coherence in presenting the brand to the consumer. Therefore, the theme of the stores opening had aroused the interest of scholars since the end of the nineties, when Fernie et al. (1997); Fernie, Moore, and Lawrie (1998) and Moore et al. (2000) focused on luxury fashion companies and showed how fundamental stores, in particular flagship stores, are to the international development of such companies. This is particularly true not only because each store becomes a point of contact with the final consumer and the local context but also because of the role that each store plays from a learning point of view because of its embeddedness in local cultures and consumption habits. As Currah and Wrigley (2004) discussed, a store can be considered a center of innovation, embedded in and necessarily shaped by a unique place.

When luxury fashion firms open stores in foreign markets, a strategic decision concerns the retail format. The following are the most common retail formats of luxury fashion companies: the flagship store and the self-standing store.[1] The flagship store is of large dimensions, localized in prestigious, internationally well-known areas, and is marked by a strong brand image that refers to the company (Arrigo, 2015). This type of store implies vast investments in the store's realization and communication and strongly links the brand with the shopping experience. Fernie et al. (1998) highlight the loss-making nature of many of these stores, making them a particularly fascinating market entry method. They observe that "flagship stores are maintained to act as publicity vehicles for the ranges and are not required to show a typical return on investment" (p. 373). The flagship store is usually owned by the company and directly managed (Wigley et al., 2012). Kozinets et al. (2002) identify three characteristics of flagship stores as follows: (1) they carry only a single brand of a product; (2) they are company-owned; and (3) they operate intending to build brand image rather than solely to generate profit for the company. Nobbs, Moore, and Sheridan (2012) add other characteristics, namely "its scale and size which usually exceeds functional need; it is derived and built on the twin features of exclusivity and uniqueness; it seeks to offer the customer a justification for their visit. The format evolves and adapts to find new ways of generating and communicating differentiation" (Nobbs et al., 2012, p. 920). Scholars have studied the flagship stores as an appropriate market entry method, especially in the case of luxury fashion companies, for their commercial role, for being a communication tool of the luxury brand and a privileged place of interaction with the customer, as well as for its being vital to the development of the fashion brand's reputation (Moore & Doherty, 2007; Moore et al., 2010). While luxury fashion companies may enter foreign markets via wholesaling at an initial stage, their internationalization process is usually marked by opening a flagship store in a prestigious location (Moore et al., 2000). The self-standing store is another retail format commonly used by luxury fashion companies. It is a smaller store (usually between 50 and 200 sq. m.) located on the shopping streets or in shopping centers, whose image

[1] Other retail formats very common in the textile and clothing sector are, for example, multi-brand stores, boutiques, department stores, factory outlets and outlet centers. For a taxonomy of retail formats, see Runfola (2012, p. 87).

is aligned with the brand policies; may be owned or in franchising, directly or third-party operated store.

The empirical research, in particular in the Italian fashion system (that is the empirical context of analysis of this study), carried on by the author and other researchers in the field, has shown that the opening of stores falls deeper and deeper into the practices of companies (Guercini & Milanesi, 2016), although the slowdown of recent years and the sharp drop that occurred in 2020 due to the pandemic and the increasingly significant weight of the digital channels. As underscored by Hutchinson, Quinn, Alexander, and Doherty (2009) and confirmed by the following studies (Moore & Doyle, 2010; Phau et al., 2014; Donzé, 2018; Cabigiosu, 2020; Armitage & Roberts, 2021), most studies have focused mainly on the internationalization of large companies. However, other types of companies develop a significant presence in foreign markets through the opening of stores, such as manufacturing SMEs (Runfola, 2012). More generally, the opening of directly operated stores seems to be an overall strategy in fashion, pursued not only by companies whose origins lie in apparel manufacturing but also by companies that entered the market via the route of the production of semi-finished textile products. More specifically, many contributions have examined luxury players in the fashion industry, adopting the perspective of large and well-known global brands managed by large multinationals, such as Prada (Moore & Doyle, 2010), LVMH (Cavender & Kincade, 2014), or Gucci (Moore & Birtwistle, 2005; Cabigiosu, 2020). However, luxury fashion SMEs and family businesses seem to have received less attention (for more details about the type of luxury fashion companies are leading domestic and foreign market players nowadays, see next chapter). Guercini and Runfola (2015a) show that the opening of stores in foreign markets is a market entry mode adopted by a variety of companies in terms of size and characteristics, such as SMEs and family businesses, which often combine manufacturing and retailing capabilities.

Through the opening of stores, many luxury fashion companies, including SMEs, manage to reach culturally and geographically distant markets, as are the emerging markets (Guercini & Milanesi, 2017). Such an operation requires acquiring market knowledge and specific retailing skills and capabilities, which can be costly, especially for SMEs, given their limited size and resources. Companies find themselves in a unique, unfamiliar geographical and cultural setting. So why do luxury fashion companies, be they large or small, decide to invest in the opening of stores even in so distant markets geographically and culturally? A first possible explanation is that despite being difficult, such a step is, in any case, deemed necessary for the future survival of the firm, especially when consumption in the domestic market is experiencing a crisis. A second explanation concerns the fact that growth through the opening of stores can favor more rapid internationalization in culturally distant markets, where a robust retail presence may signify a strong foreign presence.

Milanesi (2020) tries to analyze the motivation behind the internationalization of luxury fashion companies through the opening of stores. The author analyzed the case of large and small luxury fashion companies and found out that the reasons are quite the same for all companies: the desire to exploit the opportunities in an economically attractive foreign market, despite its distance. Luxury fashion companies view international growth as part of their proactive business philosophy of continuously searching for new opportunities. The opening of retail stores in foreign markets does not depend on the consumption crisis in the domestic market, as a reactive motivation may suggest. In other words, the approach is primarily proactive, driven by the will to obtain profit growth by exploiting a trading formula with an international appeal. The decision to internationalize through store openings also depends on some facilitating factors, including the global mindset and international orientation of the entrepreneur and managers, previous international experience (these two factors are particularly relevant for SMEs), business relationships in foreign markets, assistance and support by institutions in the domestic market.

Business relationships with relevant actors in foreign markets are crucial for opening stores in foreign markets, especially in the geographically and culturally distant ones, as business partners act as gatekeepers to facilitate entry into foreign markets (Guercini & Runfola, 2010). A related issue concerns store ownership and management. Very often, flagship stores are wholly owned and directly managed by the firm. However, there are also frequent cases concerning self-standing stores, especially located in emerging markets, in which luxury fashion companies rely on local partners through franchising or other agreements to overcome some of the difficulties attributable to foreignness and outsidership (see the last section of this chapter). Milanesi (2020) classified the opening of stores in foreign markets by luxury fashion companies into three categories. In the *internal-driven openings*, the process of store openings is driven by the will to exploit opportunities in foreign markets, and it begins with the selection of foreign markets considered suitable to the value proposition of the firm; unless it is decided to enter directly, the company takes the initiative in searching for a foreign partner. In *external-driven openings*, the process of store openings is driven by a foreign partner's unsolicited initiative. It begins with the potential foreign partners that contact the company and proposes a business opportunity in a foreign country as the target market for the opening. This process can be attributable to luxury fashion companies with a strong brand identity in domestic and foreign markets. Finally, there are *conversion-driven openings*. In this case, the process of store openings is driven by a multi-brand store that changes into a single-brand store. The process begins with the company selling products to multi-brand stores abroad, which gradually become loyal until the company's products become the majority of the store assortment; the decision to convert from a multi-brand to a single-brand store is mainly managed through franchising agreements or other forms of partnership. This type of opening often happens when the company has reached a strong brand identity and is well-known among customers in a foreign country, thanks to other sales channels, such as the digital one.

An interesting case of opening luxury fashion stores abroad is Stefano Ricci, a Florentine luxury fashion brand founded in 1972.[2] Nowadays, the company is one of the world's top players in luxury menswear, with an offer of a full range of products entirely made in Italy—some of them are made in Florence—with valuable raw materials. Stefano Ricci started with a collection of ties made with precious materials and, in 1974, following the demand of international customers, the company developed a collection of shirts, matching the ties, obtaining great success in Italy and abroad. During the 1980s, Stefano Ricci entered the US market by opening a small showroom in New York, and, in the early 1990s, the company

[2] https://www.stefanoricci.com/

decided to invest in retail operations, opening directly controlled flagship stores. This choice reflected the need to gain greater visibility and a more substantial presence in foreign markets, establish the brand worldwide and build an image of absolute elegance, luxury, and good Italian taste in clothes. Thus, the opening of stores in foreign markets represents a pillar of value creation. Stefano Ricci has developed the penetration of foreign markets through three main channels: the *multi-brand stores* (exclusive agreements with historic stores, located in exclusive locations with international and loyal customers), the *flagship stores*, directly owned and managed or opened through agreements with local partners, and the *department stores* (such as Neiman Marcus, Bergdorf Goodman, and Harrods). The first flagship store was opened in Shanghai in 1993, with a strategic vision of China's role for luxury brands. Many prestigious locations were chosen for other openings, such as Monte Carlo and Rodeo Drive in Beverly Hills. A second Chinese boutique was opened in 2002 in Beijing, inside the St. Regis Hotel, followed by the first licensed shop in the city of Chengdu. Other stores opened in that period were in Porto Cervo, Italy, in one of the most exclusive resorts of Costa Smeralda, and in Xi'an, which was the third owned flagship store in China. Two local partners were also granted the right to open licensed flagship stores in Moscow on the prestigious Bolshaya Dmitrovka, and in Paris, on Avenues des Champs-Elysees. The company's growth in foreign markets continued over the years, with sixty-eight stores all over the world in 2020. The opening of stores has always been considered a driver of growth by the company, which allows coming into direct contact with the final customer, offering a customized product, improving the global image of the brand through prestigious locations and a professional sales service, and improving the visibility and the luxury image of the product. This strategy, combined with creativity, use of precious materials, and entirely Italian production, led the company—still a family business—to exceed 150 million euros in turnover in 2018, over 95% in foreign markets.

3.3 Supply Chain and Sourcing Strategies by Luxury Fashion Companies

The efforts of luxury fashion companies in the retail side are one relevant aspect of the international growth, alongside other marketing efforts related to brand positioning and communication. However, luxury fashion companies' supply chain and sourcing strategies play an essential role in configuring the luxury offer (Christopher, 2007; Caniato et al., 2011). For all companies, not only the luxury ones, supply chain management is critical to compete in local and international markets and to ensure the delivery of products whose characteristics should match customer requirements. Moreover, there should be an alignment between the supply chain strategy and the critical success factors in the target market. Caniato et al. (2011) identified a set of critical success factors for competing in the luxury market: premium quality, craftsmanship, exclusivity, brand building, style and design, emotional appeal, country of origin, uniqueness, performance, and innovation, and lifestyle creation. The supply chain management concerns decisions about the supply chain configuration, namely the number, role, and location of the actors engaged in different processes (sourcing, manufacturing, and distributing), and the management practices related to each configuration. The supply chain configuration relates, for example, to the number of tiers, the number of actors in each tier, and their geographical dispersion (local vs. global) (Shen, Minner, Chan, & Brun, 2020).

As shown in the previous section, the downstream section of the supply chain of luxury fashion companies is often very short as they prefer to sell their products directly through their branded retail stores, thereby bypassing any kind of wholesaler or distributor. This allows luxury fashion companies to firmly control the retailing phases to reach the final customers directly. This process implies that retailing competencies are more and more a factor of competitive advantage (Guercini & Runfola, 2004). Different types of companies dominate more in general, the downstream section of the supply chain. Large, specialized retail firms and brand-dominated firms do not limit their activities to distribution; instead, they project the collection and dominate the R&D functions and the outsourcing of textiles. That is to say, they take over some of the functions that are typical of the apparel industry. There are also manufacturing firms that develop a significant retail presence by opening stores in foreign markets (Milanesi, 2020). Thus, there are forms of vertical integration in which the manufacturers gradually assume some features that are typical of the retailers, or, conversely, the retailers integrate functions of the manufacturers, assuming the characters typical of the "industrial retailer", namely "the figures of the retailer who integrates industrial capabilities (sourcing of semi-finished textiles, apparel design, product branding)" (Guercini, 2004, p. 330).

The upstream section of the supply chain may have different configurations, but high-quality products must always be guaranteed. Therefore, even if several tiers of suppliers and outsourcers exist, sourcing must ensure high-quality raw materials and semi-finished products, and the manufacturing process must be compliant with the high-quality standard. For luxury fashion companies, materials have to be sourced in those countries that guarantee top quality (e.g., leather in Italy, alpaca in Peru, cashmere in China and Mongolia).

Brun et al. (2008) found that luxury companies keep the most critical production phases in-house, such as the cutting phase, and only the non-critical and labor-intensive phases, such as sewing, can be outsourced, with a careful selection of suppliers and strict monitoring of their operations. As shown by Guercini and Milanesi (2019), some manufacturing phases are locally outsourced to suppliers in the same industrial district that can be considered as an "external" production department, often totally dedicated to one main focal company through close and long-lasting relationships, as in the case of Gucci and the first-, second-, and third-tier suppliers all located in the Florentine leather district. However, especially during the last two decades, lead firms in luxury fashion value chains have also adopted offshore outsourcing of the manufacturing phases to a global network of suppliers (Fernie & Azuma, 2004). Even the requirements of retail stores abroad (e.g., delivery times, product customization) may lead luxury fashion companies to reinforce business relationships with critical suppliers, with whom there is mutual dependence.

It must also be noted that a critical success factor of a luxury product is the country of origin, so the production phases, even when outsourced, take place in the same country of the focal company, especially for luxury fashion companies that have a strong image and reputation for luxury production all over the world, such as Italy and France. Additionally, the management of global supply chains poses operational challenges and increases costs, so that many companies have started to reconfigure their value chains through facility relocation and changes of the supply bases back to their home country (Ancarani et al., 2015). This phenomenon is defined as reshoring, namely the return of production activities back to the company's home country, regardless of the ownership of the relocated activities (Ellram et al., 2013). Some UK luxury brands (e.g., Burberry, Barbour, and Mulberry) were among the first to have reshored part of their manufacturing processes to their home country to re-establish the brand authenticity and country of origin in response to increasing demand for British-made luxury fashion items. Robinson and Hsieh (2016) list many factors that impact luxury brand supply chains and justify the reshoring by luxury companies: shortened product lifecycles, raw material procurement costs, pressure on margins, lack of control in the outsourced manufacturing process, the need to quickly track their merchandise and ensure control of quality and inventory accuracy, streamlining safety, compliance auditing, the need to manage product recalls, minimize counterfeiting risk and other threats to brand authenticity. The European Monitor of Reshoring surveyed 165 cases of European companies in 2014–2017 that made the reverse path to relocation, bringing within the national borders productions previously outsourced elsewhere. In this sample, Italian and English companies dominate, followed by French. The leading sector of this productive relocation is undoubtedly fashion, particularly luxury, which has registered the most significant cases of reshoring in recent years. Among these there are brands such as Prada, Ferragamo, Ermenegildo Zegna, Bottega Veneta, Geox, Benetton, Piquadro, and Nannini. The reasons behind the return to Italy are the poor quality of offshore production, delivery times, and customers' sensitivity to the coherence between brand country and product made in.

3.4 The Role of e-Commerce for Internationalization

Luxury fashion companies have focused on opening physical stores for years, but in more recent years, they have begun to invest in e-commerce and virtual spaces (Guercini & Runfola, 2015b). However, many luxury fashion companies have been skeptical of recreating the luxury bricks-and-mortar experience into a digital world, supporting the idea that digital platforms do not allow to maintain the same exclusivity of physical stores and, therefore, brand identity (Balasyan & Casais, 2018). Even scholars have questioned the relationship between digital and luxury. Okonkwo (2009) argued that the uniqueness of luxury goods is incompatible with digital channels, which, by definition, are aimed at a mass market, and there is also the problem of lack of physical contact with the products and their sellers. Similarly, Dennis, Fenech, and Merrilees (2004) highlighted the sensory nature of luxury goods because human senses are imperative when selling luxury goods.

Moreover, luxury is more related to passion than reason (Okonkwo, 2016), with elements of originality and creativity that concern the product and the retail conceptualization, which can be better created through physical stores that can deliver an exclusive and unique purchase (Dion & Arnould, 2011). There is also another adverse issue related to luxury goods sold online, namely counterfeiting. As concluded by Hennigs, Wiedmann, and Klarmann (2012), a luxury company selling all its products online reveals all the details of its collection and, therefore, nurtures the market of fakes. All these reasons justify the skepticism and distrust of luxury companies in using the Internet and online sales channels (Hennigs et al., 2012; Klugeaa et al., 2013).

However, especially in the last decade, the significantly increased use of the Internet as a shopping medium has broken down luxury fashion companies' resistances, which are now focusing on developing their online presence and pushing online sales (Kim, 2013). Data from consulting companies also confirm this trend. The COVID-19 crisis accelerated online sales for luxury companies, with the share of purchases made online that nearly doubled from 12% in 2019 to 23% in 2020. Moreover, online is expected to become the leading channel for luxury purchases by 2025, with younger generations (Millennials and Generation Z) as leading actors in online purchases (Bain & Company, 2020).

Additionally, the Internet has been recognized as an entry mode into international markets, which can be associated with the international development of large companies and SMEs (Pezderka & Sinkovics, 2011). In particular, Internet and online sales allow companies to pursue internationalization and open to "the conduct of business transactions across national boundaries, where the crossing of national boundaries takes place in the virtual rather than in the real or spatial domain" (Yamin & Sinkovics, 2006, p. 359). The online presence transcends international boundaries and enables consumers from almost all over the world to get in touch with a company and eventually buy its products (Premazzi et al., 2010). Sinkovics, Sinkovics, and "Bryan" Jean, R.J. (2013) address the Internet as a path of internationalization suitable for SMEs to enhance their export performance. Also, an online presence can enhance the speed of internationalization (Hassouneh & Brengman, 2011). Thus, besides physical stores, the Internet is another channel that can be used by luxury fashion companies both as a communication tool and transaction site (Riley & Lacroix, 2003; Nyeck & Roux, 2003). E-commerce represents an opportunity for luxury fashion brands to sell to consumers who do not have easy access to the traditional channel (Kapferer, 2000). Indeed, some luxury companies sell through third-party e-commerce platforms, including multi-brand online retailers such as Farfetch, Mytheresa, Luisa Via Roma (Guercini et al., 2020), besides their exclusive website. In other words, the trade-off between a digital presence and luxury seems to be overcome, as evidenced by some large luxury fashion companies, such as Prada and Versace, which, after years of refusal, have strongly developed a digital presence in recent years. The beneficiaries of this are mainly the new generations of luxury consumers, as they are showing an increasing preference for the online channel to purchase luxury products (Dauriz et al., 2014; Lee, Rothenberg, & Xu, 2020), especially young consumers from emerging markets (Ngai & Cho, 2012).

The use of an e-commerce platform (the company website or a third-party one) is combined with the offline channel, namely directly operated stores, third-parties-operated stores, and, albeit to a much lesser extent, multi-brand stores, one channel complementing the other. Moreover, the online channel includes other digital tools, such as the mobile e-commerce app and social media, which can also be used for social commerce (Huang & Benyoucef, 2013). Therefore, the success of online internationalization depends on the integration between online and offline channels, according to an omnichannel approach, namely a synergetic management of the different channels and customer touchpoints to deliver a consistent customer experience across channels (Ozuem & Azemi, 2017). Thus, from an omnichannel perspective, the challenge now is to manage all the touchpoints to convey a unique brand identity and a valuable brand experience. A recent contribution by Silva, Duarte, and Sundetova (2020) highlights how fashion and apparel brands are adopting an omnichannel approach, with differences between low-cost, mid-price, and luxury brands, even if with many points in common. Low-cost brands, such as H&M and Mango, use several online and offline channels, including the following seven: store, catalog, website, blog, newsletter, mobile app, and social networks. Much attention is given to the website, with specific characteristics: user-friendly navigation and accessibility from many countries; updated product and price information; several options of product delivery, return, and payments; in-store availability option; live chat; and links to social networks. An example of integrating online and offline channels is represented by the option "click and collect" to deliver products to the nearest store. As for the social networks (Instagram, Facebook, YouTube, Twitter, and Pinterest), they provide detailed product descriptions and prices (especially on Instagram), link to the website, videos with campaigns, vlogs, interviews, and fashion shows. A high degree of channel integration is also testified by the features of the mobile application that, as in the case of H&M, includes in-store assistance to find the right color or size of an item when the customer goes to the physical store and a "Scan and Find" function that allows finding a product online using a barcode from the price tag. Mid-priced brands, such as Guess and Massimo Dutti, use the same seven channels and have "click and reserve" services that allow consumers to reserve the product online and pay and collect in the physical store. Even the use of social media and mobile applications is quite similar to low-cost brands. Luxury brands, such as Gucci and Burberry, show similar characteristics and a high degree of integration, especially between mobile applications and websites (Silva et al., 2020).

To sum up, on the one hand, luxury fashion companies should develop a digital transformation that incorporates their website, dynamic and user-friendly e-commerce, a strategic presence in social networks, and the development of an overall digital marketing strategy (Guercini et al., 2020a; Guercini et al., 2020b). On the other hand, a priority of luxury fashion companies is the integration of digital technologies in their stores in domestic and foreign markets, as the physical store, although the temporary closures due to the COVID-19 pandemic, still plays—and will play—an essential role for customers who want to live an exciting, offline shopping experience (Arrigo, 2018; Aiolfi & Sabbadin, 2019; Alexander & Cano, 2020). As Becagli and Milanesi (2021) discussed, the contingent aspects of the COVID-19 pandemic require a rethinking of the management of the mix of retail channels, with the online channels having a leading role in supporting sales in domestic and foreign markets. Social distancing, limits to the fitting of products, especially fashion goods in physical stores, reduction of the capacity of stores linked to social distancing rules, psychological aspects related to the fear of contagion, a general feeling of insecurity, seem to undermine the traditional preference for the physical store. These changes will probably produce a profound transformation of consumers' purchasing habits, which will not necessarily see the total abandonment of the physical store but will probably promote a rethinking of its function within the omnichannel approach.

Adopting a multi-channel approach and the investment in an e-commerce website represent a path undertaken by well-established Italian luxury fashion companies. Luisa Spagnoli is an interesting example.[3] Luisa Spagnoli has a long tradition in womenswear, with more than eighty years of history. Established in Perugia in 1928, the company is still family owned and represents an interesting case for international expansion and the opening of retail stores abroad. Luisa Spagnoli history began around 1928 thanks to the founder's entrepreneurial spirit, a woman with great creativity and entrepreneurial orientation. The

[3] https://www.luisaspagnoli.it/it_it/storia-1.html

company was the first to introduce the use of angora yarn to produce knit garments, and over the years, it has played a primary role in boosting the industrial development of the Umbria region. This historical women's prêt-à-porter brand, which was one of the first to develop through a network of directly managed boutiques, opened the e-commerce website in 2015, accessible in all countries of the European Union, Great Britain, the Balkans, Switzerland, South Africa, Australia, and the United States. Luisa Spagnoli also opened the e-store to reach markets where she is not yet present, for example, France. In addition, the e-store also served as a test for the American and Australian markets, the brand's target markets.

Another example is Furla, an Italian luxury goods company founded by the Furlanetto family in 1927. The company features Italian-designed products that range from handbags and shoes to accessories. In the 1990s, after Bologna, Rome, and Paris, the store on Madison Avenue in New York was opened as the first step of a far-sighted distribution network covering no less than sixty-three foreign markets, from Europe to Asia and the United States. In late 2008, the company also inaugurated its pan-European web boutique and another international expansion plan that included opening major flagship stores in Rome, London, Hong Kong, and Beijing. Furla is very attentive to Millennials and Gen Z because they represent the customers of the future. The company is investing heavily in digital and has an e-commerce website that records year-on-year increases (+43% in 2019 compared to the previous year). Japan is confirmed as the first market for the brand at a geographical level, thanks to a consolidated relationship with that market that has lasted since the 1990s.[4]

3.5 Liabilities in Internationalization

The Internet and online sales cannot be considered a panacea, especially for internationalization, as their potential can vary from country to country due to restrictions (Zaheer & Manrakhan, 2001), logistics challenges

[4] https://www.milanofinanza.it/news/furla-l-e-commerce-vola-a-43-nel-2019-202002201725551175

related to the geographical distance and its costs (Overby & Min, 2001). Additionally, there may be structural and political constraints in Internet use, such as in China, where Google and Facebook are not available, that may inhibit a company's push for internationalization or require adaptation to the local digital tools (Jin, 2012). In other words, the availability of the Internet beyond national borders does not eliminate all forms of distance and liabilities that companies may face in their internationalization process (Johanson & Vahlne, 2009; Sinkovics et al., 2013). Liabilities in internationalization can be defined as difficulties faced by companies in their internationalization process, and only in part concern the digital context but, above all, they manifest in the internationalization of companies both through the opening of subsidiaries and in the opening of stores in foreign markets. Within the international business domain, Johanson and Vahlne (2009) discuss the difficulties in the internationalization process in terms of the shift from the liability of foreignness to the liability of outsidership, where the first is linked to the concept of psychic distance and the second has to do with networks and relationships.

The liability of foreignness (LOF) is a well-known concept developed in the international business literature, initially conceptualized by Hymer (1976) as the "costs of doing business abroad". LOF deals with the fact that foreign firms incur additional costs when operating at an international level, compared to local firms that have better information and knowledge about their country, economy, laws, culture, politics, and so on. In 1995, Zaheer introduced the concept of "liabilities of foreignness" and its four constituent categories: (1) costs due to the spatial distance between the parent company and the subsidiaries; (2) costs incurred exclusively by foreign subsidiaries due to unfamiliarity with the host country's environments; (3) costs due to economic nationalism and lack of legitimacy in the host country; and (4) costs from sales restrictions imposed by the home country. The debate on the conceptualization, operationalization, and measurement of liability of foreignness has continued over the years in the international business domain and is still open. A relevant contribution is provided by Eden and Miller (2001) and their two hazards that affect foreign firms disproportionately to local firms in the host country: unfamiliarity hazards, which concern the lack of knowledge of or experience in the host country and place foreign firms at a disadvantage compared to local firms; discrimination hazards, which consist of the discriminatory treatment inflicted on foreign firms in the host country by the home or host governments or by consumers. There is broad consensus on the relationship between LOF and psychic distance. In particular, Johanson and Vahlne (2009) relate LOF to the construct of psychic distance, arguing that "internationalization frequently started in foreign markets that were close to the domestic market in terms of psychic distance, defined as factors that make it difficult to understand foreign environments. The companies would then gradually enter other markets that were further away in psychic distance terms. … This process had its origin in the liability of foreignness. … The larger the psychic distance the larger is the liability of foreignness" (Johanson & Vahlne, 2009, p. 1412). The two authors also recognized the importance of relational hazards in the sense that, in a network view, network ties in the foreign market are an effective means to overcome the liability of foreignness (Rangan & Drummond, 2004; Cuervo-Cazurra et al., 2007). Thus, another relevant liability in internationalization is the liability of outsidership (LOO) that comes with information constraints and uncertainties regarding network development and opportunities that emerge in business relationships (Hilmersson, 2013). As discussed by Johanson and Vahlne (2009) in their revised Uppsala model of internationalization, firms need to gain trust from and develop relationships with members of a network to get the status of an insider. Otherwise, there is a liability of outsidership. LOO manifests in situations in which companies enter a business environment, both domestic and foreign, without knowing the business actors and how they are related to each other. Being involved in one or several business relationships in a business environment guarantees a position of insidership, which is necessary to get access to market knowledge and successfully develop a business in a host country (Li & Fleury, 2020).

Other liabilities may occur, such as the liability of newness (LON) and the liability of smallness (LOS), related to organizational age and size. LON originates in the organizational theory and organizational ecology research (Stinchcombe, 1965) and refers to the fact that young organizations have a higher propensity to die than old organizations because they cannot compete with established organizations and have low levels of legitimacy. Organizational ecologists often discuss LON in connection with the liability of smallness (Aldrich & Auster, 1986; Brüderl & Schüssler, 1990). LOS refers to the limitedness of resources and capabilities that may generate vulnerability to environmental changes. Size can be measured in terms of financial capital or the number of employees (Hannan & Freeman, 1984). LON and LOS represent key challenges to manage in the domestic market, but they may also occur in the internationalization process, becoming a suffering and complicating factor, additional to foreignness and outsidership.

And what about liabilities for luxury fashion companies? Research in this field is limited. Brannen (2004), when discussing liabilities and assets related to foreignness, maintain that foreignness can be an asset in the case of luxury goods with inimitable and highly recognized brand names and country of origin that allow capitalizing on foreignness. Another contribution in this field is that of Milanesi (2020), who analyzed the liabilities that luxury fashion companies encounter when they open stores in foreign markets, often with the support of a foreign partner. She concluded that the problems of foreignness and outsidership are not disjoint but must be addressed simultaneously. In the case of luxury fashion companies, the relationship with a partner for foreign market entry is relevant to overcome the psychic distance to the market and build relationships with other actors, such as local institutions or with other potential partners.

Similarly, the author shows that without a local partner, luxury fashion companies cannot enter psychically and geographically distant markets, such as Russia or China. Guercini and Milanesi (2017) observed that the internationalization process of luxury fashion companies, especially the most exclusive ones—the so-called extreme luxury fashion companies—is directed to those niches of consumers in geographically and culturally distant markets from the beginning of the international expansion, through a rapid rush of internationalization of retail activities. For such companies, foreignness becomes an asset, an advantage related to the value of the perception of the home country in the destination country. In particular, a specific home country, such as Italy, in a specialized field, that of luxury fashion in which Italy is one of the leading countries, mitigates LOF and turns it into an asset, reducing also the need to adapt the offer for international markets, with positive implications on the overall cost of the internationalization process.

References

Aiolfi, S., & Sabbadin, E. (2019). Fashion and new luxury digital disruption: The new challenges of fashion between omnichannel and traditional retailing. *International Journal of Business and Management, 14*(8), 41–51.

Aldrich, H., & Auster, E. R. (1986). Even dwarfs started small: Liabilities of age and size and their strategic implications. *Research in Organizational Behavior, 8*, 165–198.

Alexander, B., & Cano, M. B. (2020). Store of the future: Towards a (re) invention and (re) imagination of physical store space in an omnichannel context. *Journal of Retailing and Consumer Services, 55*, 101913.

Alleres, D. (2003). *Competing marketing strategies of luxury fashion companies*. Adapted, translated and cited in M. Bruce & C. Kratz. Elsevier Butterworth-Heinemann.

Ancarani, A., Di Mauro, C., Fratocchi, L., Orzes, G., & Sartor, M. (2015). Prior to reshoring: A duration analysis of foreign manufacturing ventures. *International Journal of Production Economics, 169*, 141–155.

Armitage, J., & Roberts, J. (2021). The globalisation of luxury fashion: The case of Gucci. *Luxury, 6*(3), 1–20.

Arrigo, E. (2015). The role of the flagship store location in luxury branding. An international exploratory study. *International Journal of Retail & Distribution Management, 43*(6), 518–537.

Arrigo, E. (2018). The flagship stores as sustainability communication channels for luxury fashion retailers. *Journal of Retailing and Consumer Services, 44*, 170–177.

Bain & Company. (2020). *The future of luxury: Bouncing back from Covid-19*. Available at https://www.bain.com/insights/the-future-of-luxury-bouncing-back-from-covid-19/

Bakir, A., Gentina, E., & de Araújo Gil, L. (2020). What shapes adolescents' attitudes toward luxury brands? The role of self-worth, self-construal, gender and national culture. *Journal of Retailing and Consumer Services, 57*, 102208.

Balasyan, I., & Casais, B. (2018). Keeping exclusivity in an E-commerce environment: The case of Farfetch.com and the market of luxury clothes. *International Journal of Marketing, Communication and New Media, 4*, 6–27.

Becagli, C., & Milanesi, M. (2021). Omnichannel retailing and brand equity: A new balance to achieve. In W. Ozuem & S. Ranfagni (Eds.), *The art of digital marketing for fashion and luxury brands. Market spaces and marketplaces*. Palgrave Macmillan.

Berridge, H. S. (2018). A practical look at the challenges luxury fashion brands face in the wake of digitalization: Is it time that luxury fashion brands learn to love e-commerce platforms? *Journal of Intellectual Property Law & Practice, 13*(11), 901–908.

Brannen, M. Y. (2004). When Mickey loses face: Recontextualization, semantic fit, and the semiotics of foreignness. *Academy of Management Review, 29*(4), 593–616.

Bruce, M., & Kratz, C. (2007). Competitive marketing strategies of luxury fashion companies. In Hines, T. & Bruce, M. (Eds.) *Fashion marketing: Contemporary issues*, 130–150.

Brüderl, J., & Schüssler, R. (1990). Organizational mortality: The liabilities of newness and adolescence. *Administrative Science Quarterly, 35*(3), 530–547.

Brun, A., Caniato, F., Caridi, M., Castelli, C., Miragliotta, G., Ronchi, S., … Spina, G. (2008). Logistics and supply chain management in luxury fashion retail: Empirical investigation of Italian firms. *International Journal of Production Economics, 114*(2), 554–570.

Cabigiosu, A. (2020). *Digitalization in the luxury fashion industry*. Springer International Publishing.

Caniato, F., Caridi, M., Castelli, C., & Golini, R. (2011). Supply chain management in the luxury industry: A first classification of companies and their strategies. *International Journal of Production Economics, 133*(2), 622–633.

Castelli, C. M., & Brun, A. (2010). Alignment of retail channels in the fashion supply chain. An empirical study of Italian fashion retailers. *International Journal of Retail & Distribution Management, 38*(1), 24–44.

Cavender, R., & Kincade, D. H. (2014). Leveraging designer creativity for impact in luxury brand management: An in-depth case study of designers in the Louis Vuitton Möet Hennessy (LVMH) brand portfolio. *Global Fashion Brands: Style, Luxury & History, 1*(1), 199–214.

Cavusgil, S. T., & Buckley, P. J. (2016). Interdisciplinary perspectives on the middle class phenomenon in emerging markets. *International Business Review, 3*(25), 621–623.

Chandon, J. L., Laurent, G., & Valette-Florence, P. (2016). Pursuing the concept of luxury: Introduction to the JBR special issue on luxury marketing from tradition to innovation. *Journal of Business Research, 69*(1), 299–303.

Christopher, M. (2007). New directions in logistics. In D. Walters (Ed.), *Global logistics*. Kogan Page Limited.

Christopher, M., Lowson, R., & Peck, H. (2004). Creating agile supply chains in the fashion industry. *International Journal of Retail & Distribution Management, 32*(8), 367–376.

Corbetta, G., Minichilli, A., & Quarato, F. (2015). *VIII Osservatorio AUB sulle aziende familiari italiane*. AUB.

Craig, C. S., & Douglas, S. P. (2000). Configural advantage in global markets. *Journal of International Marketing, 8*(1), 6–26.

Cuervo-Cazurra, A., Maloney, M. M., & Manrakhan, S. (2007). Causes of the difficulties in internationalization. *Journal of International Business Studies, 38*(5), 709–725.

Currah, A., & Wrigley, N. (2004). Networks of organizational learning and adaptation in retail TNCs. *Global Networks, 4*(1), 1–23.

Dauriz, L., Remy, N., & Sandri, N. (2014). *Luxury shopping in the digital age. Perspectives on retail and Consumers Goods*. Available at: https://www.mckinsey.com/industries/retail/our-insights/luxury-shopping-in-the-digital-age

Dennis, C., Fenech, T., & Merrilees, B. (2004). *E-Retailing*. Routledge.

Dion, D., & Arnould, E. (2011). Retail luxury strategy: Assembling charisma through art and magic. *Journal of Retailing, 87*(4), 502–520.

Donzé, P. Y. (2018). The birth of luxury big business: LVMH. In Richemont & Kering (Eds.), *Global Luxury* (pp. 19–38). Palgrave.

Eden, L., & Miller, S. (2001, August). Opening the black box: Multinationals and the costs of doing business abroad. In *Academy of Management Proceedings*, 1, C1-C6, Briarcliff Manor, NY 10510: Academy of Management.

Ellram, L. M., Tate, W. L., & Petersen, K. J. (2013). Offshoring and reshoring: An update on the manufacturing location decision. *Journal of Supply Chain Management, 49*(2), 14–22.

Fernie, J., & Azuma, N. (2004). The changing nature of Japanese fashion. *European Journal of Marketing, 38*(7), 790–808.

Fernie, J., Moore, C., Lawrie, A., & Hallsworth, A. (1997). The internationalization of the high fashion brand: The case of Central London. *Journal of Product & Brand Management, 6*(3), 151–162.

Fernie, J., Moore, C. M., & Lawrie, A. (1998). A tale of two cities: An examination of fashion designer retailing within London and New York. *Journal of Product & Brand Management, 7*(5), 367–378.

Fionda, A. M., & Moore, C. M. (2009). The anatomy of the luxury fashion brand. *Journal of Brand Management, 16*(5), 347–363.

Godey, B., Manthiou, A., Pederzoli, D., Rokka, J., Aiello, G., Donvito, R., & Singh, R. (2016). Social media marketing efforts of luxury brands: Influence on brand equity and consumer behavior. *Journal of Business Research, 69*(12), 5833–5841.

Guercini, S. (2004). International competitive change and strategic behaviour of Italian textile-apparel firms. *Journal of Fashion Marketing and Management, 8*, 320–339.

Guercini, S., & Milanesi, M. (2016). Store openings and sourcing strategies in the internationalization on fashion industrial retailers. In A. Vecchi & C. Buckley (Eds.), *Handbook of research on global fashion management and merchandising* (pp. 374–397).

Guercini, S., & Milanesi, M. (2017). Extreme luxury fashion: Business model and internationalization process. *International Marketing Review, 34*(3), 403–424.

Guercini, S., & Milanesi, M. (2019). Understanding changes within business networks: Evidences from the international expansion of fashion firms. *Journal of Business & Industrial Marketing, 34*(1), 192–204.

Guercini, S., Milanesi, M., Mir-Bernal, P., & Runfola, A. (2020a). Surfing the waves of new marketing in luxury fashion: The case of online multibrand retailers. In F. J. Martínez-López & S. D'Alessandro (Eds.), *Advances in digital marketing and ecommerce*. Springer Proceedings in Business and Economics.

Guercini, S., Ranfagni, S., & Runfola, A. (2020b). E-commerce internationalization for top luxury fashion brands: Some emerging strategic issues. *Journal of Management* Development, *39*(4), 423–436.

Guercini, S., & Runfola, A. (2004). Sourcing strategies in clothing retail firms: Product complexity versus overseas supply chain. *Journal of Customer Behaviour, 3*(3), 305–334.

Guercini, S., & Runfola, A. (2010). Business networks and retail internationalization: A case analysis in the fashion industry. *Industrial Marketing Management, 39*(6), 908–916.

Guercini, S., & Runfola, A. (2015a). Small-medium sized manufacturers' internationalization through retail store openings abroad: A study of the Italian fashion industry. In *International Marketing in the Fast Changing World*. Emerald Group Publishing Limited.

Guercini, S., & Runfola, A. (2015b). Internationalization through e-commerce. The case of multibrand luxury retailers in the fashion industry. *Advances in International Marketing, 26*, 15–31.

Guercini, S., & Runfola, A. (2016). Lo sviluppo nel retail come modalita'di internazionalizzazione delle PMI manifatturiere. *Il caso della moda. Piccola Impresa/Small Business, 1*, 37–53.

Guercini, S., & Runfola, A. (2019). Developing fashion retail operations to growth in emerging markets. *Journal of Global Fashion Marketing, 10*(2), 145–162.

Hannan, M. T., & Freeman, J. (1984). Structural inertia and organizational change. *American Sociological Review, 49*, 149–164.

Hansen, T., & Jensen, J. M. (2009). Shopping orientation and online clothing purchases: The role of gender and purchase situation. *European Journal of Marketing, 43*(9/10), 1154–1170.

Hassouneh, D., & Brengman, M. (2011). Virtual worlds: A gateway for SMEs toward internationalization. *Journal of Brand Management, 19*(1), 72–90.

Hennigs, N., Wiedmann, K. P., & Klarmann, C. (2012). Luxury brands in the digital age – Exclusivity versus ubiquity. *Marketing Review St. Gallen, 29*(1), 30–35.

Hilmersson, M. (2013). The effect of international experience on the degree of SME insidership in newly opened business networks. *Baltic Journal of Management, 8*(4), 397–415.

Hines, T., & Bruce, M. (2007). *Fashion marketing*. Routledge.

Huang, Z., & Benyoucef, M. (2013). From e-commerce to social commerce: A close look at design features. *Electronic Commerce Research and Applications, 12*(4), 246–259.

Hutchinson, K., Quinn, B., Alexander, N., & Doherty, A. M. (2009). Retailer internationalization: Overcoming barriers to expansion. *The International Review of Retail, Distribution and Consumer Research, 19*(3), 251–272.

Hymer, S. H. (1976). *The international operations of national firms. A study of direct foreign investment*. MITPress.

Jackson, T. (2004). A contemporary analysis of global luxury brands. *International Retail Marketing, 1*, 155–169.

Jin, B., & Cedrola, E. (2016). Overview of fashion brand internationalization: Theories and trends. In *Fashion brand internationalization* (pp. 1–30). Palgrave Pivot.

Jin, S. A. A. (2012). The potential of social media for luxury brand management. *Marketing Intelligence & Planning, 30*(7), 687–699.

Jin, S. V., Ryu, E., & Muqaddam, A. (2021). I trust what she's# endorsing on Instagram: Moderating effects of parasocial interaction and social presence in fashion influencer marketing. *Journal of Fashion Marketing and Management, 25*(4), 665–681.

Johanson, J., & Vahlne, J. E. (2009). The Uppsala internationalization process model revisited: From liability of foreignness to liability of outsidership. *Journal of International Business Studies, 40*(9), 1411–1431.

Kapferer, J. N. (2000). *How the internet impacts on brand management.* Springer.

Kapferer, J. N., & Bastien, V. (2012). *The luxury strategy: Break the rules of marketing to build luxury brands.* Kogan Page Publishers.

Kapferer, J. N., & Tabatoni, O. (2011). Are luxury brands really a financial dream? *Journal of Strategic Management Education, 7*(4), 1–16.

Kim, A. J., & Ko, E. (2012). Do social media marketing activities enhance customer equity? An empirical study of luxury fashion brand. *Journal of Business Research, 65*(10), 1480–1486.

Kim, S. (2013). A classification of luxury fashion Brands' E-commerce sites. *Journal of Fashion Business, 17*(6), 125–140.

Kluge, P. N., Königsfeld, J. A., Fassnacht, M., & Mitschke, F. (2013). Luxury web atmospherics: An examination of homepage design. *International Journal of Retail & Distribution Management, 41*(11/12), 901–916.

Kozinets, R. V., Sherry, J. F., DeBerry-Spence, B., Duhachek, A., Nuttavuthisit, K., & Storm, D. (2002). Themed flagship brand stores in the new millennium: Theory, practice, prospects. *Journal of Retailing, 78*(1), 17–29.

Kulmala, M., Mesiranta, N., & Tuominen, P. (2013). Organic and amplified eWOM in consumer fashion blogs. *Journal of Fashion Marketing and Management, 17*(1), 20–37.

Lee, H., Rothenberg, L., & Xu, Y. (2020). Young luxury fashion consumers' preferences in multi-channel environment. *International Journal of Retail & Distribution Management, 48*(3), 244–261.

Li, J., & Fleury, M. T. L. (2020). Overcoming the liability of outsidership for emerging market MNEs: A capability-building perspective. *Journal of International Business Studies, 51*(1), 23–37.

Liu, S., Perry, P., Moore, C., & Warnaby, G. (2016). The standardization-localization dilemma of brand communications for luxury fashion retailers' internationalization into China. *Journal of Business Research, 69*(1), 357–364.

Milanesi, M. (2020). *Liabilities and networks in the internationalization of fashion retailing.* FrancoAngeli.

Milanesi, M., Guercini, S., & Tunisini, A. (2020). Exploring SMEs' qualitative growth and networking through formalization. *Competitiveness Review, 30*(4), 397–415.

Mir-Bernal, P., Guercini, S., & Sádaba, T. (2018). The role of e-commerce in the internationalization of Spanish luxury fashion multibrand retailers. *Journal of Global Fashion Marketing, 9*(1), 59–72.
Moore, C. (1998). L'internationalisation du prêt-à-porter: The case of Kookai and Morgan's entry into the UK fashion market. *Journal of Fashion Marketing and Management, 2*(2), 153–158.
Moore, C., & Birtwistle, G. (2005). The nature of parenting advantage in luxury fashion retailing – The case of Gucci group NV. *International Journal of Retail & Distribution Management, 33*(4), 256–270.
Moore, C., & Burt, S. (2007). Developing a research agenda for the internationalization of fashion retailing. In T. Hines & M. Bruce (Eds.), *Fashion marketing: Contemporary issues* (pp. 68–85). Elsevier Butterworth Heinemann.
Moore, C., & Doherty, A. M. (2007). The international flagship stores of luxury fashion retailers. In T. Hines & M. Bruce (Eds.), *Fashion marketing: Contemporary issues* (pp. 277–296). Elsevier Butterworth Heinemann.
Moore, C., Doherty, A. M., & Doyle, S. A. (2010). Flagship stores as a market entry method: The perspective of luxury fashion retailing. *European Journal of Marketing, 44*(1), 139–161.
Moore, C., Fernie, J., & Burt, S. (2000). Brands without boundaries – The internationalisation of the designer retailer's brand. *European Journal of Marketing, 34*(8), 919–937.
Moore, C. M., & Doyle, S. A. (2010). The evolution of a luxury brand: The case of Prada. *International Journal of Retail & Distribution Management, 38*(11/12), 915–927.
Newman, A., & Cullen, P. (2002). *Retailing: Environment & operations*. Cengage Learning EMEA.
Ngai, J., & Cho, E. (2012). The young luxury consumers in China. *Young Consumers, 13*(3), 255–266.
Nobbs, K., Moore, C. M., & Sheridan, M. (2012). The flagship format within the luxury fashion market. *International Journal of Retail & Distribution* Management, *40*(12), 920–934.
Nyeck, S., & Roux, E. (2003). Valeurs culturelles et attitudes par rapport au luxe: l'exemple du Québec. In *Association Sciences Administration Canada, Conférence annuelle de l'ASAC,* 14–17, Halifax, NS, Canada.
Okonkwo, U. (2016). *Luxury fashion branding: Trends, tactics, techniques.* Springer.
Okonkwo, U. (2009). Sustaining the luxury brand on the internet. *Journal of Brand Management, 16*(5–6), 302–310.

Overby, J. W., & Min, S. (2001). International supply chain management in an internet environment. *International Marketing Review, 18*(4), 392–420.

Ozuem, W., & Azemi, Y. (Eds.). (2017). *Digital marketing strategies for fashion and luxury brands*. IGI Global.

Pezderka, N., & Sinkovics, R. R. (2011). A conceptualization of e-risk perceptions and implications for small firm active online internationalization. *International Business Review, 20*(4), 409–422.

Phau, I., Teah, M., Cavender, R., & Kincade, D. H. (2014). Management of a luxury brand: Dimensions and sub-variables from a case study of LVMH. *Journal of Fashion Marketing and Management, 18*(2), 231–248.

Premazzi, K., Castaldo, S., Grosso, M., Raman, P., Brudvig, S., & Hofacker, C. F. (2010). Customer information sharing with e-vendors: The roles of incentives and trust. *International Journal of Electronic Commerce, 14*(3), 63–91.

Rangan, S., & Drummond, A. (2004). Explaining outcomes in competition among foreign multinationals in a focal host market. *Strategic Management Journal, 25*(3), 285–293.

Riley, F. D. O., & Lacroix, C. (2003). Luxury branding on the internet: Lost opportunity or impossibility?. *Marketing Intelligence & Planning 21*(2), 96–104.

Robinson, P. K., & Hsieh, L. (2016). Reshoring: A strategic renewal of luxury clothing supply chains. *Operations Management Research, 9*(3), 89–101.

Romão, M. T., Moro, S., Rita, P., & Ramos, P. (2019). Leveraging a luxury fashion brand through social media. *European Research on Management and Business Economics, 25*(1), 15–22.

Rovai, S. (2018). Digitalisation, luxury fashion and "Chineseness": The influence of the Chinese context for luxury brands and the online luxury consumers experience. *Journal of Global Fashion Marketing, 9*(2), 116–128.

Runfola, A. (2012). *Apprendimento e reti nei processi di internazionalizzazione del retail. Il caso del tessile e abbigliamento*. Florence University Press.

Runfola, A., Ranfagni, S., & Guercini, S. (2018). The internationalization of Italian luxury brands. The Missoni case. In *Contemporary case studies on fashion production, marketing and operations* (pp. 73–88). Springer.

Shen, B., Minner, S., Chan, H. L., & Brun, A. (2020). Logistics and supply chain management in the luxury industry. *Transportation Research Part E: Logistics and Transportation Review, 143*, 102095.

Shukla, P. (2012). The influence of value perceptions on luxury purchase intentions in developed and emerging markets. *International Marketing Review, 29*(6), 574–596.
Silva, S. C., Duarte, P., & Sundetova, A. (2020). Multichannel versus omnichannel: A price-segmented comparison from the fashion industry. *International Journal of Retail & Distribution Management, 48*(4), 417–4130.
Sinkovics, N., Sinkovics, R. R., & "Bryan" Jean, R. J. (2013). The internet as an alternative path to internationalization? *International Marketing Review, 30*(2), 130–155.
Stinchcombe, A. L. (1965). Social structure and organizations. In J. G. March (Ed.), *Handbook of organizations* (pp. 142–193). Rand McNally.
Tavoletti, E. (2011). The internationalization process of Italian fashion firms: Looking for an analytical generalization. *South Asian Journal of Management, 18*(2), 7–29.
Vickers, J. S., & Renand, F. (2003). The marketing of luxury goods: An exploratory study–three conceptual dimensions. *The Marketing Review, 3*(4), 459–478.
Wigley, S., & Moore, C. M. (2007). The operationalisation of international fashion retailer success. *Journal of Fashion Marketing and Management, 11*(2), 281–296.
Wigley, S. M., Moore, C. M., & Birtwistle, G. (2005). Product and brand. *International Journal of Retail & Distribution Management, 33*(7), 531–544.
Wigley, S. M., Sinha, P., Nobbs, K., Moore, C. M., & Sheridan, M. (2012). The flagship format within the luxury fashion market. *International Journal of Retail & Distribution Management, 40*, 920–934.
Yamin, M., & Sinkovics, R. R. (2006). Online internationalisation, psychic distance reduction and the virtuality trap. *International Business Review, 15*(4), 339–360.
Zaheer, S. (1995). Overcoming the liability of foreignness. *Academy of Management Journal, 38*(2), 341–363.
Zaheer, S., & Manrakhan, S. (2001). Concentration and dispersion in global industries: Remote electronic access and the location of economic activities. *Journal of International Business Studies, 32*(4), 667–686.

4

The International Dimension of the Luxury Fashion Business Models

4.1 Business Model Conceptualization: The Need for an International Perspective in Luxury

This chapter aims to understand how internationalization represents one of the main components of the business models of companies in luxury fashion. Both empirical pieces of evidence and theoretical debate emphasize the emergence of different models in the luxury industry. This chapter concentrates the attention on such business models, focusing on companies that manage directly or indirectly manufacturing processes. Hence, the analysis will not consider the business models of pure luxury retailers. However, this does not imply that luxury companies having a manufacturing nature do not invest in retailing, as already stated in previous chapters. Hence, while the previous chapters answered *why* luxury players are international, focusing on the motives, and *how* they implement internationalization, looking at the strategies, this chapter deepens the implications for business models in luxury fashion and their international features.

A. Runfola et al., *Internationalization of Luxury Fashion Firms*, Palgrave Advances in Luxury, https://doi.org/10.1007/978-3-030-88755-1_4

Hence, it is essential to understand the interplay between internationalization and the business model. As already pointed out in this book, the luxury industry has an international vocation regarding supply markets and final consumers. Nevertheless, to what extent do theoretical contributions consider internationalization issues within the business model domain?

To answer this question, we have to recall the concept of the business model, how the literature defines it, and the main areas of study within the management literature. As it is well known, the term "business model" is widely used both by academics and managers (Warnier & Runfola, 2014). Moreover, the term entered the managerial dictionary to explain how companies do business (Teece, 2018). In particular, the business model terminology has received greater attention during the last two decades, considering the impact of new waves of competition within the business environment. The Internet's growth has led to the emergence of digital business models (Zott et al., 2010).

Moreover, new trends about corporate social responsibility (CSR) have favored the rise of initiatives that relate business models with sustainability issues including ecological, social, and economic impacts (Massa et al., 2017). As a result, we have witnessed new companies that make sustainability the distinctive feature of their model and the transition of traditional business models toward "sustainable" business models. This trend involved all sectors, including fashion. Accordingly, for-profit and non-profit companies propose new ways of offering fashion products (Todeschini et al., 2017; Runfola et al., 2020).

To summarize, business models can explain the conduct of a variety of companies in a diversity of sectors, selling products as well as services (see, e.g., Runfola et al., 2013).

However, what exactly means the term "business model" is far from being commonly shared among scholars. According to Teece (2010), one of the prominent experts in the field, it relates to how companies define their value offering (*value creation*), deliver this value to the market (*value delivery*), and turn it into profits (*value capture*). Therefore, the business model is a rather broad concept that includes many company activities, from the organizational to the manufacturing and commercial ones. Within the managerial debate, the business model has not found a universally valid and accepted definition or interpretation. In general, there is a close relationship between the business model and the strategies implemented by companies (Casadesus-Masanell & Ricart, 2010). The effectiveness of company policies depends on the business model. So the two terms are connected while not synonymous. In the attempt of systematizing the now pervasive literature on the business model, Massa et al. (2017) propose a taxonomy of the meaning of "business model". They highlight three prevailing conceptualizations.

The first interpretation considers business models as "*attributes of real firms*" (Massa et al., 2017, p. 76). According to this interpretation, the business model relates to the empirical and real world that has given rise to a series of modus operandi, representing competitive benchmarks. To support this, the authors list some business models' archetypes, such as the "razor and blade" or the "freemium" models. The second interpretation conceptualizes the business model as a "*cognitive/linguistic schema*" (Massa et al., 2017, page 76), emphasizing how the term interplays with managers' perceptions. Following this idea, it must be considered the managers' cognition of how the business model works and should work, rather than the formal structuring. The third and final interpretation considers the business models as "*formal conceptual representations of how an organization functions*" (Massa et al., 2017, page 76), which refers to the possibility of representing business models through visual schemes (such as diagrams) rather than describing through specific templates what a business model is.

Similarly, within the literature, there is no consensus about the components of the business model. As Foss and Saebi (2017) highlight, the business model represents a series of interrelated subsystems or components that interact with each other to create, deliver, and capture value. Among the various contributions that have focused attention on the dimensions that constitute a business model, one of the most frequently used templates is the Canvass business model proposed by Osterwalder and Pigneur (2010). It is a well-known scheme, widely diffused in the empirical world, and tries to capture the essence of the business model, identifying the components that characterize it. In particular, according to the authors, nine dimensions describe a business model: the target consumer segments, the value proposition, the communication and distribution channels, the types of relationships with customers, the revenue model, the total costs associated with the model, the key activities and related resources and skills, the partnerships. The Canvass business model has been used to represent the business models of well-known companies and a valuable template for intervening on individual components and proposing changes. Within the academic debate, we can identify more theoretically derived conceptualizations of business model components. One example is the contribution of Demil and Lecocq (2010). The two authors adopt a Penrosian view (from the seminal contribution of Edith Penrose), following a resource-based approach to business models. In particular, they highlight three main components of a business model (Demil & Lecocq, 2010, p. 234): the resources (tangible and intangible) and the competencies (including the core ones), which the company can combine; the organization dimension, in terms of how the company manages the value network and relationships with external actors; the value propositions and, therefore, the types of products and services offered. These three elements, which the authors identify together with the acronym resources and competences, organization, value propositions (RCOV), allow scholars and managers to understand how to ensure the model's efficiency and effectiveness.

To sum up, the management literature is fascinated by the business model concept and its definition. This area has recently also given rise to a new line of research that specifically concerns the study of business model innovation (Schneider & Spieth, 2013). To systematize the literature, Foss and Saebi (2017) highlight how business model innovation is a research stream that is different from the traditional literature on the business model, stating how change requires ad hoc contributions. The authors identify two combining dimensions for business model change: "scope" and "novelty". The "scope" can regard the entire architecture or only some of the components (module), while the "novelty" can be for the company or the whole business.

Four archetypes of business model innovation are defined (Foss & Saebi, 2017, p. 217). Regarding the modular scope, the authors identify the "evolutionary business model" and "focus business model innovation".

Concerning the architectural scope, the authors consider the "adaptive business model innovation" and "the complex business model innovation".

Therefore, the issues related to the business model and business model innovation characterize management studies. In this scenario, how does internationalization fit? It does not represent one of the components specifically considered part of the prevailing literature's business model. Internationalization indeed refers to a strategy that companies can implement but not a component of the business model. Some contributions point out the role that business model innovation has for international expansion. For example, Rask (2014) identifies four types of business models according to an international perspective. The author shows differences in designing the business model emerging from the consideration of the geographical dimension. At the same time, the author's contribution posits the lack of studies of internationalization concerning the business model theoretical domain. However, as highlighted in the previous chapters, in the business model of luxury fashion companies, the international dimension represents one of the critical characteristics capable of characterizing all the components (Guercini and Milanesi, 2017). From this point of view, this chapter intends to deepen how internationalization represents a dimension of the company's business model, which enables it to generate value, transfer it to the market, and contribute to profitability. Figure 4.1 below shows our line of reasoning.

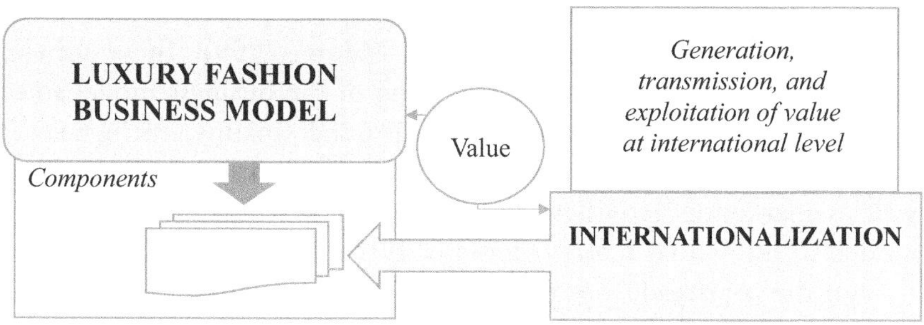

Fig. 4.1 The luxury business model and the international dimension. (Source: Authors' elaboration)

4.2 Problematizing Business Models in the Luxury Fashion

How to identify business models in the luxury fashion industry? Furthermore, to what extent does the internationalization dimension represent a component of the business model innovation? It is not easy to answer these questions. Traditionally, according to Kapferer and Bastien (2009), it is assumed that there is substantially one way to build an effective business model in luxury fashion. In particular, luxury companies should implement some common strategies that derive from some rules to follow. Kapferer and colleagues (Kapferer & Bastien, 2009; Kapferer, 2012a) define the so-called "anti-laws of marketing" that must guide the configuration of the business model of luxury companies. In this respect, some indications are provided, such as maintaining complete control over the supply chain and the distribution channels, non-use of licenses, selective distribution, and not to use advertising (Kapferer & Bastien, 2009).

According to the author's perspective, companies that aspire to emerge in the luxury sector should try to set up a series of strategies capable of isolating them from a competitive standpoint. In fact, as Kapferer states, "the luxury business model aims at creating incomparability, which grants freedom to set one's own prices. In contrast, in all other business models, prices are set while taking the competition's prices into account" (Kapferer, 2012b, p. 59). Similarly, there is no shortage of literature contributions highlighting the importance of some features that the luxury brand should possess, such as exclusivity, heritage, and prestige price (Fionda & Moore, 2009). These are elements capable of guiding the structuring of the business model since they influence every area relating to the product, manufacturing activities and sourcing processes, the supervision of distribution channels, as well as marketing activities, and which allow studying the business models of individual actors (Moore & Birtwistle, 2004).

Over the last decade, however, some pillars related to the luxury business model have changed. Take, for example, how the Internet revolutionizes distribution in the luxury market (Guercini & Runfola, 2015). Furthermore, the current global pandemic scenario has implications that can have disruptive effects on the business models of luxury companies. According to D'Arpizio and Levato (2020) from Bain & Company, five significant trends characterize the current context for luxury companies and impact the structuring of the business model. They are: (a) the shift toward local purchases, due to the reduction in travel that has resulted in significant purchases for customers at the national level; (b) the pervasive role of Generation Z, which becomes the protagonist of the luxury market; (c) the prevalence of the digital channel in the purchasing of fashion items; (d) the rethinking of the role of the physical retail store, with the need to proceed with processes of rationalization of the network of stores; (e) the changing role of the luxury brand, with the growing importance of contents and their transmission to the market. Furthermore, we should point out that the concept of business model can be considered firm-specific. Therefore, each company can propose a different mix of business model components.

Both the empirical world and previous academic contributions allow us to outline the existence of a plurality of business models in the luxury industry. These models are proposed in this chapter by explicitly considering the role of internationalization. As highlighted by Runfola and Guercini (2013), resources and assets of the business model fuel the international expansion. In luxury fashion, this means fueling a global dimension, as highlighted in previous chapters. However, internationalization requires resources, investments, ad hoc strategies. As a result, internationalization puts the business model under tension and calls for change and innovation. The answer that companies can give to this depends on the specific business model configuration. In the continuation of this chapter, we briefly describe these business models, highlighting how the international dimension fits and characterizes their dimensions. Based on this, we propose below the analysis of four business models of luxury fashion companies (see Fig. 4.2): business models of large luxury fashion MNEs; independent entrepreneurial luxury SMEs; vertically integrated luxury suppliers; digital native luxury brands.

4.3 Business Models of Luxury Fashion MNEs

The first type of business model is that of large MNEs. Although single players are different, we can include within this typology all business models of large companies with a global scale presence, both in production and selling markets. These companies manage well-known brands at an international level. Within this macro-typology, it is possible to include large conglomerate companies (such as LVMH, Kering, Richemont), and MNEs with established brands, such as global players of French origin (e.g., Chanel or Hermès), Italian (e.g., Prada, D&G, and Armani), American (e.g., Ralph Lauren or Michael Kors) and British (e.g., Burberry and Stella McCartney). The management literature has extensively studied the business models of these companies (see, e.g., Moore & Doyle, 2010).

Moreover, they have been the subject of attention from global research and consultancy institutes (Bain & Company, McKinsey & Company,

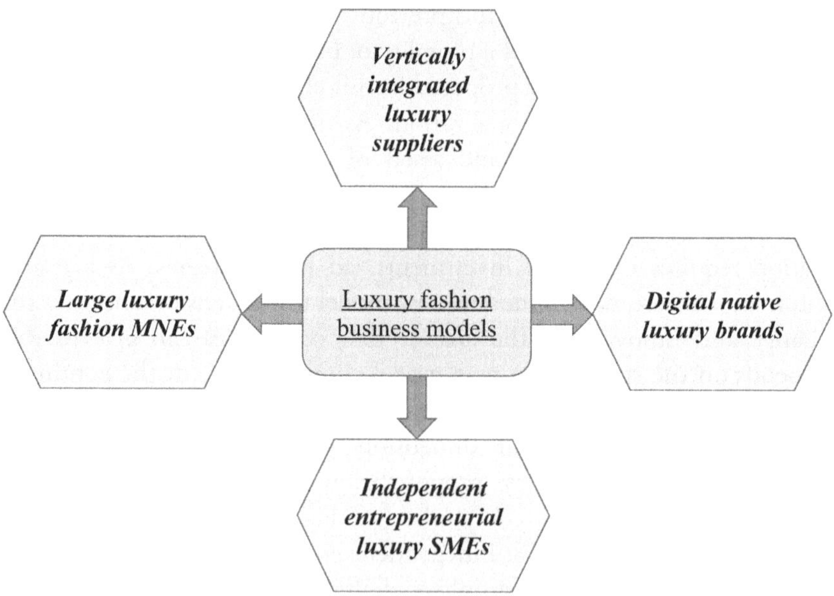

Fig. 4.2 Four types of luxury fashion business models. (Source: Authors' elaboration)

Boston Consulting Group, Deloitte, to name a few). Large luxury multinationals have a well-defined product portfolio, a global brand image, direct supervision of retail activities, and complete management of international value chains. As a result, consulting firms include these companies in the rankings as top leading players in luxury.

Large conglomerate luxury groups, including LVMH, Richemont, and Kering, play a primary role in the global luxury scenario. Deloitte (2020), for example, highlights that in 2019, LVMH (with about 37,468 million dollars of luxury goods sales) represents the first player in global luxury, followed by Kering (with about 17,777 million dollars of luxury goods sales), while Richemont (with 13,833 million dollars sales of luxury goods sales) ranks fourth. Donzé (2018), who analyzes similarities and differences among these three companies, points out that the large luxury conglomerate groups represent the competitive benchmark for all the other players in the luxury business. Beyond the differences in value propositions, such as the various product categories covered, these three companies, through high financial resources, have heavily invested in communication to support branding policies and implement mass production policies and global presence in terms of retail store development. The development of retail activities has been fundamental for expanding in foreign markets. As highlighted in the previous chapter, the opening of single-brand stores for many fashion companies represents a means to approach the new luxury markets in developing countries. According to Guercini and Runfola (2019), in fact, "following the global manufacturing shift, we are now witnessing a shift in wealth, which also involves a shift of stores as direct channels for the brands of manufacturing firms in emerging markets" (p. 13). The luxury MNEs have been protagonists of this path. Similarly, these players have implemented development paths in e-commerce internationalization, even through partnerships. For example, in 2020, Farfetch and Alibaba, the two leading players in the online channel worldwide, signed a partnership with Richemont that aimed to speed up the digitalization and develop further in the Chinese market.[1]

---

[1] https://s22.q4cdn.com/426100162/files/doc_news/2020/11/Farfetch-Alibaba-and-Richemont-form-Global-Partnership.pdf

British and US companies are other luxury MNEs that characterize this business model typology. However, as Doyle and Moore (2018) highlight, compared to French or Swiss multinationals, dominant in business, they do not have a conglomerate nature. The two authors underline that the decision to avoid diversification has highlighted other specific dimensions of the strategic orientations of these companies. For example, in terms of value proposition, Doyle and Moore (2018) underline that British players are focused on the "heritage of country living" (p. 81), while the Americans rely on the "heritage of sportswear" (p. 81). Some of these players invest heavily in digitalization. According to Guercini et al. (2020b), Burberry has a massive e-commerce presence in the leading luxury markets, both mature and emerging. Over the years, Burberry has achieved high levels of omnichannel orientation, integrating both retail stores and e-commerce platform in the top ten country markets in terms of luxury sales. The study shows that the omnichannel orientation at an international level is not easy and the British luxury player represents a strategic benchmark.

As already pointed out, within the business models of luxury MNEs we can include Italian-based companies. They lever Made in Italy, creativity, and craftsmanship as competitive advantages about their value proposition. To name a few, players such as Prada, Armani, D&G, and Salvatore Ferragamo are symbols of Made in Italy and globally recognized for their positioning. However, the Italian luxury sector has been the subject of acquisitions in the last decades by foreign MNEs companies. For example, in 2018, the well-known brand Versace was acquired by the American company Michael Kors for roughly 1.83 billion Euros (Pambianconews, 2018a). Similarly, French companies have set up acquisitions, such as the 2-billion acquisition in 2013 of Loro Piana, a luxury textile company, by LVMH,[2] or the acquisition of Gucci by Kering Group at the end of the 1990s.

Beyond the differences that can be traced back to individual companies, the business models of large luxury players show some shared features. Therefore, the international dimension is inherent in these players

---

[2] https://st.ilsole24ore.com/art/finanza-e-mercati/2013-07-09/lvmh-compra-loro-piana-064623.shtml (accessed 26/05/2021).

and permeates all the business model components. Figure 4.3 shows the business model's main international characteristics. They relate to the ability to impose luxury fashion trends worldwide, global brand awareness, the leading roles in global value chains, and the considerable investments in foreign distribution channels and media coverage. In addition, these features regard both offline and online development.

The current competitive context and the COVID-19 pandemic have forced luxury MNEs to rethink some building blocks of their business model. Considering the 23% reduction of the personal luxury goods market in 2020 due to the pandemic crisis (D'Arpizio et al., 2021), some of the main assets of the luxury MNEs business model are under tension. For example, the temporary closure of retail stores or the reduced sales from traveling consumers (travel retail) lead to difficulties in delivering the value proposition through traditional channels, asking for more massive marketing digital tools. Furthermore, from a production point of view, the international configuration of supply chains is in question due to lockdowns that imposed some restrictions to suppliers' activities in some countries. Hence, the COVID-19 pandemic seems to have accelerated some change trends (such as digitalization or reshoring) already affecting the luxury market, as shown in the previous chapters. For example, rethinking how to configure international supply chains was not a

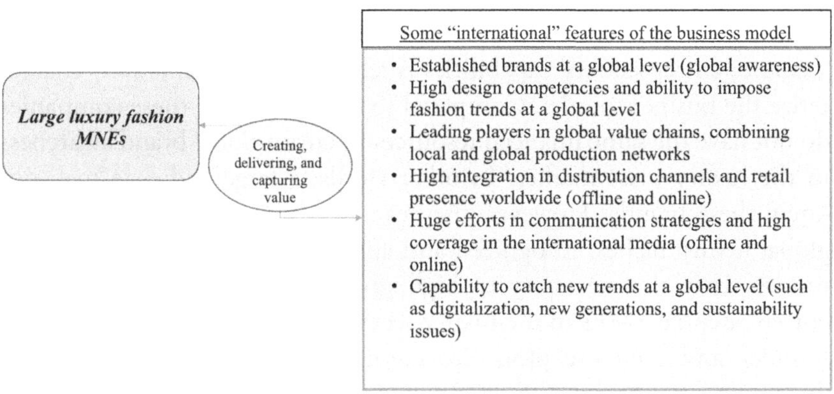

Fig. 4.3 The identity card of the luxury fashion MNEs. (Source: Authors' elaboration)

new issue since it emerged before the pandemic. Robinson and Hsieh (2016) highlight the reshoring process undertaken, for example, by Burberry. To preserve the value of Britishness and authenticity, the company has "relocating manufacturing activities performed by offshore suppliers (e.g. trench coat licensee in Germany) back to wholly owned domestic-based facilities in the Castleford factory" (p. 98). Therefore, these and other questions permeate the change in the business model of luxury fashion MNEs, whose business model still represents a reference point for all the other companies in the sector.

4.4 Business Models of Independent Entrepreneurial Luxury SMEs

The second business model is that of independent firms with an entrepreneurial nature and small-medium size. Within this typology, the entrepreneur plays an important role. Entrepreneurial companies base much of their international success on the ability of the business decision-maker, the entrepreneur, to develop strategies on how to approach foreign markets and meet customers' requirements (Guercini & Runfola, 2021a). SMEs internationalization is frequently associated with the "effectuation logic" proposed in the academic field by Sarasvathy (2001). According to this approach, decision-makers start from the available resources to delineate the most suitable strategies to implement. In this scenario, entrepreneurs' capabilities (such as market orientation) characterize the business model. Compared to luxury MNEs, these companies do not have the same financial resources to create global brand awareness in the luxury mass market. In other words, a large audience may not know these brands. However, they can still become leading brands in global luxury niches, recognized and appreciated by specific target customers. It is also necessary to highlight another fascinating aspect of entrepreneurial SMEs in the luxury sector. The entrepreneur is often the founder (and, therefore, progenitor) or member of a generation of a family running the business. Sometimes, families have been managing the companies for many decades. Hence, the business model of SMEs in luxury intertwines with the family business domain. In this regard, some authors showed the specificity of family business models as a form of SMEs business models (Gamble et al., 2021). The founder and the need to manage generational transitions influence the business model (Gamble et al., 2021).

In other words, the founder gives an imprint to the company, which subsequent generations take into account and over time represents a value that the family helps to generate and keep alive; however, it is the generational shift itself that represents a moment of crisis for this model. In general, family businesses largely contribute to Western economies. Scholars have recently studied internationalization methods and family business' ability to enhance the identity and heritage dimension and connection with the territory from which they come (Baù et al., 2017; Ranfagni et al., 2018). Ranfagni et al. (2021), for example, elaborate on the concept of authenticity to explain how family firms exploit their local roots to internationalize. Considering the role of the heritage from local systems in the luxury fashion industry, we may consider the case of Naples in Italy. Naples has a strong heritage in craftsmanship and sartorial traditions within the fashion production. It is also a well-recognized Italian city at a global level. In this context, companies leverage knowledge and territorial roots to propose worldwide well-known brands. For example, we can mention E.Marinella, a specialized brand in the production of the ties,[3] or Kiton, a leading player in the luxury industry, especially for menswear.

Many luxury companies in the fashion system have a family origin, with the family having a primary role for the positioning in foreign markets. In many cases, the brand name follows a patronymic approach (Olivares-Delgado et al., 2016), with the name of the family being the company's brand (Kashmiri & Mahajan, 2010). Giacosa (2014) highlights that family businesses in luxury have peculiar characteristics. The author stresses the role of corporate heritage and long-term vision as distinctive features. The long-term vision is a fundamental characteristic of these companies' business models and can grant a stronger connection to the company's family values and past strategies. Differently, a short-term

[3] An extended case study of E.Marinella will be provided in Chap. 5.

vision may be more oriented to profits and then lead to a managerial approach that could also imply sudden changes in the company's management.

Among family companies in this business model typology, the example of luxury SMEs in Italy is noteworthy. The Italian context shows a variety of SMEs operating in the luxury sector. Luxury family companies characterize all sectors of Made in Italy productions. Thus, we can find examples in the design/furniture industry or the food sector (see, e.g., the internationalization of luxury SMEs in the truffle industry proposed by Milanesi et al., 2020). Runfola et al. (2018) present an exemplificative case in this respect, the Missoni case. Missoni is a family-owned company with a long-time corporate heritage, a symbol of the traditional Made in Italy. Although it is small in size and turnover, the brand is well known at the international level. The authors discuss the main drivers that characterize its business model and guide its international development. In particular, four main building blocks foster the expansion abroad: the family as a unifying force for all activities; the integration of both communication and distribution channels; a complex set of values that characterize the brand beyond the Made in Italy, and the search for a new dimension of the brand positioning. In this case, what is important to note is that the company represents a remarkable example of how a brand could be a relevant player in the market, although with a small-medium size.

Following this example, it is important to note how this type of company may follow a business model that seems to replicate large multinational companies, although with some adaptation due to the smaller dimension. For example, in terms of internationalization, this kind of business model seems to push the company to select different international markets according to a more gradual approach (Vahlne, 2020). In other words, the internationalization process can follow an incremental path that begins from the national market and develops on less distant markets in terms of psychic distance.

There are also cases of the companies that grow internationally and acquire great notoriety worldwide, highlighting the transition from business models typical of small businesses to medium- or large-sized models.

Ranfagni and Runfola (2012), for example, propose the case of Brunello Cucinelli. Through sapient product policies, the company's approach to fashion development managed to grow and acquired an international reputation. The brand originated in the small village of Solomeo near Perugia in Italy, and it is now a well-established luxury player with a turnover that in 2019 exceeded 600 million euros, with an increase of roughly 10% compared to 2018 (Pambianconews, 2020). The company's business model refers to what the founder entrepreneur defines as "humanistic capitalism". Some building blocks of the company model are the craftsmanship and creativity of Made in Italy productions, sustainable development, healthy profitability, and exclusive positioning and distribution.[4]

Similarly, we can consider the case of the previously mentioned Kiton, a Naples-based company. Kiton is a family business, now managed by the third generation of entrepreneurs. It has a unique positioning in the luxury industry due to its extraordinary quality. The origin dates back to the 1950s of the last century, while the brand Kiton was launched in the 1960s. The company is an example of a luxury player globally known for its brand heritage, Made in Italy, and anchored to its founder's identity, Ciro Paone. Over the last decades, it has steadily grown, becoming a prominent luxury brand in the luxury menswear, with the Kiton jacket being a leading global product. In addition, the company produces womenswear and accessories. In 2019, Ciro Paone Spa that owns the brand Kiton reached roughly 135 million euros of net sales.[5] Kiton is renowned for its exclusive quality, creativity, research on fabrics, and it is recognized and appreciated by the most influential personalities in the world. It currently owns five manufacturing plants in Italy with more than 800 employees; most are tailors and artisans. It also manages a tailoring school for preserving and developing sartorial traditions and grant new generations of tailors to the company. Craftsmanship, exclusivity, innovation are all part of the company offering, whose motto is "the best of the best + 1". It now has a wide presence worldwide, covering different

[4] http://investor.brunellocucinelli.com/en/business-model/the-business-model

[5] Source: Ciro Paone Spa, "Prospetto contabile del Bilancio consolidato" closed 31-12-2019.

distribution channels in more than seventy countries, including more than fifty retail stores.[6]

At the same time, luxury SMEs also include companies that show how internationalization has been the main asset since their inception. In other words, there may be business models that have an immediate global emphasis. However, in the literature, this phenomenon received less attention in the luxury market. For example, Guercini and Milanesi (2017), studying a well-known Italian luxury company, propose the extreme luxury business model. They advance the idea of a "business model that finds full expression in culturally and geographically distant markets from the home country" (p. 416), where "internationalization being a constitutive element of the business model itself" (p. 418). Furthermore, they argue that the extreme luxury business model finds its international markets' performance by matching home country and destination markets features. In particular, Guercini and Milanesi (2017) show some critical characteristics of this business model: targets for the value proposed (namely made in production, craftsmanship, hand-made productions) are niche consumers in a global arena; the creation of the value refers to a well-defined positioning in the luxury business with the role of local manufacturing; the delivery of the value to destination markets rely on retail stores in primary locations; pricing strategies aimed at supporting an extreme luxury positioning.

Recently, even new emerging markets have proposed entrepreneurial initiatives. Significant is the case of China. Heine and Gutsatz (2015) highlight a paradox of the Chinese luxury market. While representing the primary market for luxury consumption, China does not have globally recognized luxury companies. Instead, the authors highlight that the Chinese market shows a series of entrepreneurial initiatives that have entered the luxury market to offer new business models. In particular, the authors discuss the rise of new SMEs, such as those resulting from the collaboration of Western entrepreneurs who partner with Chinese designers and new Chinese luxury companies. Gutsatz (2014) also underlines the emergence of business models having a value proposition that is the result of "design in China" but "Made in Italy". These initiatives exploit

[6] https://it.kiton.com/

assets from different places in an attempt to present new value propositions. The author describes Western brands launching Chinese brands, such as the Shang Xia brand by Hermès, and companies with multiple locations or more headquarters, where the entrepreneurial origin is less evident.

Therefore, concerning the business model of luxury independent entrepreneurial SMEs, internationalization represents an essential dimension and a challenge simultaneously. For example, retail growth processes and a direct presence in foreign markets require resources that are not necessarily available to the company. As a result, SMEs may search for partners and third-party investments. In international markets, luxury independent entrepreneurial SMEs may rely on relationships with gatekeepers that favor entry and development (Guercini & Runfola, 2010; Milanesi et al., 2020). Furthermore, as happened in Italian family businesses, being exposed to acquisition by large companies represents a risk (or even an opportunity) for these companies. In fact, large companies can be attracted by the brand potential of some luxury independent entrepreneurial SMEs and decide to invest in exploiting it globally. Consequently, SMEs may perceive a trade-off between growth, which would lead to acquisitions by or contracting with prominent players, and maintaining the small-medium size to remain independent.

Figure 4.4 below shows some international features of the business model of luxury independent entrepreneurial SMEs. As noted previously,

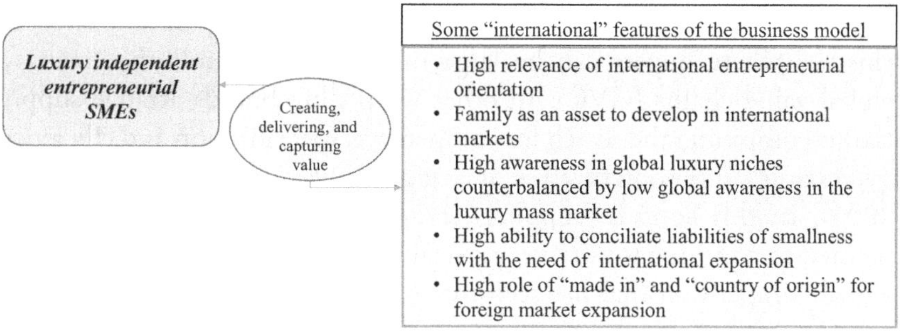

Fig. 4.4 The identity card of luxury independent entrepreneurial SMEs. (Source: Authors' elaboration)

the entrepreneurial direction is fundamental and is mainly related to a family nature. Moreover, while the company may not be known to a vast global audience, the brand is well established internationally in global niches. Hence, from an international perspective, this business model's effectiveness lies in balancing liabilities of smallness with international development. In many cases, the country of origin represents a competitive lever to exploit to grant further growth in foreign markets.

4.5 Luxury Brands of Vertically Integrated Suppliers

Alongside the companies that manage luxury brands (MNEs or SMEs) for final markets since their beginning, it is necessary to highlight the presence of business models proposed by players from the upstream levels of the fashion supply chain and whose origin is in B2B markets. The fashion industry offers possibilities in terms of integration along the supply chain. Several actors may follow the road of proposing their collections, even though they come from the initial stages of the pipeline. For example, yarn or fabric producers may start apparel production in the textile-clothing supply chain and set up a new brand name to relate with final consumers.

In this scenario, therefore, we propose the business model of vertically integrated suppliers. Most of the production of luxury products takes place in the interplay between buyer-supplier in global-local value chains. Suppliers can be players at a local level, such as companies located in clusters, where buyers can be large international brands that manage global value chains (GVC). In other words, big brands arrange supply chains combining the search for competence/specialization and efficiency by mixing supply alternatives at a global level (Guercini & Runfola, 2004). In this context, suppliers should rethink the strategies implemented to continue to survive, especially considering the emergence of a global competition that has seen the shift in production from high-cost factor markets toward new production countries. In fashion, this phenomenon has given rise for decades to outsourcing and offshoring phenomena globally (Gereffi, 2001) and to the emergence of a GVC in which individual players (typically buyers) become dominant players.

Once again, the case of Italy is emblematic of this phenomenon. As clearly highlighted by Achille and Zipser (2020) in a McKinsey report, about 40% of luxury production occurs in Italy in small family businesses that operate as subcontractors for prominent players. These companies have their location in industrial districts, where knowledge about the production of various types of luxury products is established. The industrial districts represent a model of industrialization in Italy, object of studies concerning how the local aggregation of small supplier companies operate in international contexts. In addition, these companies have also become a symbol and bearers of the typical values of Made in Italy, such as craftsmanship and high specialization. The ability of these companies to offer manufacturing skills and high levels of knowledge has made them productive partners of large luxury groups over time. There are also examples of large luxury companies, which decided to permanently place their presence in the districts with their organizational units, to have direct contact with suppliers, or in any case, to capture the added value inherent in the specific location. Significant in this sense is the case of the Florentine leather goods district. It is a "leather valley" of luxury items where over 4500 companies produce bags, shoes, leather goods. Over time, big players such as Richemont, LVMH, Burberry, Gucci, and Prada, to name a few (Pambianconews, 2018b), have invested in this area. In these contexts, the prominent luxury players have acted by acquiring their suppliers and/or creating their production plants and offices that follow the development of the product.

Therefore, local and global supply chains combine, giving rise to a series of links between actors of different sizes and with varying manufacturing origins. Indeed, the linkages between local and global actors represent one of the core themes in the studies on the configuration and evolution of GVCs (De Marchi et al., 2017). Being part of GVCs imposes the need to constantly rethink the value configuration and the strategies through which actors manage to remain part of these systems. In general, for some decades, already in some local production contexts, not only in the world of luxury, there have been crisis phenomena that have generated tensions in the business models of subcontractors (De Marchi et al.,

2017). As a result, suppliers must adapt their business models to face the current competitive scenario and better interact with customers (Guercini & Runfola, 2021b).

Starting from inter-organizational connections (Gereffi et al., 2005), previous research has highlighted, for example, the strategies that different suppliers can put into practice to upgrade (Guercini & Runfola, 2004; Lechner et al., 2020) and their ability to provide value to lead global firms (Gereffi, 1994). In addition, the recent COVID-19 pandemic has pushed local and international players to rethink their strategies under a high degree of uncertainty. Most of the big brands tried to support their local chains to help maintain the production value put under tension by the production blocks due to the global pandemic (Runfola et al., 2021).

As already stated, local-global linkages are particularly important for suppliers located in high-cost factors countries, such as France and Italy. However, due to the competition with suppliers from emerging and developing countries, maintaining inter-firm relationships with lead global firms requires new strategies. The ability to offer high value-added products, technologically advanced production systems, and respond to new environmental sustainability requirements, are just a few of the possible strategies that also explain the resilience of suppliers in local contexts, such as those in industrial districts (De Marchi et al., 2017).

Among the various alternatives, one of the strategies implemented by these companies is to develop their branded collections. In this sense, the company can either decide to abandon the previous business or, more frequently, combine the B2B and B2C dimensions. In other words, it is a hybrid model in which two souls coexist, one on the industrial side, with the maintenance of the relationships with big players (B2B relationships), and one on the consumption side (B2C relationships) with the development of a new brand. In this regard, Depeyre et al. (2018) study the case of the French suppliers of MNEs. The study shows that one response from suppliers was to implement a "coopetition" to cooperate as a supplier of luxury brands and propose their brand. It is an emerging business model that presents some challenges, which, according to Depeyre et al. (2018), derives from the need to balance the two souls and the related tensions that can emerge and depends on the reaction of the luxury actors with whom they are in a relationship.

Similarly, some companies followed the same path in the Italian context, operating in B2B and B2C markets. We may consider the case of Lanificio Faliero Sarti. The company's location is within the industrial district of Prato, one of the biggest in Italy with a strong heritage in wool textile and garment making. Faliero Sarti is a well-known and historical company that sells high-end fabrics made with fine materials. It has clients in various international markets, including well-renowned fashion brands. The company's specialization regards "haute couture" and "prêt à porter" fabrics. The company's origin dates back to 1949, and it is still a prominent player in the textile industry. It is a family business. At the beginning of 2000, one member of the third generation of the family decided to create a collection of sophisticated luxury women's shawls, men's and women's scarves, and cashmere pashmina. The company started to sell its products through boutiques and online channels. Lanificio Faliero Sarti represents a remarkable example of how suppliers in the fashion industry can leverage product and production knowledge to explore new paths, representing a benchmark for other firms in the district.[7]

In Italy, we also find cases of aggregation of suppliers to jointly target the final consumers. For example, Guercini and Runfola (2011) propose the case of cooperating SMEs in the clothing, shoes, and leather supply chains that have created joint organizations to manage some marketing activities. In particular, through the establishment of consortia, SMEs in the luxury supply chains have integrated marketing activities, such as the decision to develop a single umbrella brand and open retail stores in foreign markets. The retail stores propose an assortment composed of a selection of all suppliers' offerings. These initiatives aimed at experimentation, which, beyond the economic-financial performance, made it possible to undertake new paths toward final markets. At the same time, downstream development allow SMEs

[7] https://www.falierosarti.com/it/about.html

to acquire new types of knowledge to spend in the relationship with their industrial partner. More than in previous business models, the internationalization dimension represents a challenge for this type of business. Companies that come from B2B markets may face high barriers in developing internationally in B2C markets. However, foreign markets knowledge may refer to skills acquired in interaction with international business customers.

Figure 4.5 summarizes some dimensions of the business model of these companies. As stated above, the international market knowledge may descend from B2B interactions. These are fundamental contexts that can grant knowledge about global trends. In addition, the business model's value proposition can rely on manufacturing competencies that have let companies emerge in B2B markets. Hence, market knowledge integrates deep product knowledge. The fact that these players come from upfront phases of the pipeline implies a reduced brand awareness. However, being "new players" from a B2C point of view lets them experiment with new ways to approach targets in international markets. Finally, it is necessary to highlight how the COVID-19 pandemic breaks into this scenario, calling for new answers and new strategies in value configuration. The pandemic may be providing these players with new opportunities for foreign markets and developing new digital technology channels.

Fig. 4.5 The identity card of vertically integrated luxury suppliers. (Source: Authors' elaboration)

4.6 Digital Natives Luxury Brands

The fourth business model combines digital and manufacturing dimensions. This typology includes business models that emerge from the advent of digital innovation and new technologies. Brands may intertwine digital opportunities with manufacturing skills. Compared to the previous ones, it is a recent phenomenon, minority in the luxury industry since it refers to new entrepreneurial initiatives, often linked to start-ups in the digital field. As pointed out in the previous chapters, e-commerce represents one of the growth areas of the world of luxury at an international level. In the current pandemic context of crisis and difficulties of the world economies, the digital channel roughly doubled its market share, as already pointed out in the previous chapters. D'Arpizio et al. (2021) from Bain & Company estimates that, in the world of personal luxury goods, online sales grew from 12% in 2019 to 23% in 2020 and should reach up to 30% by 2025.

In online luxury, it is possible to find a series of business models that primarily concern the world of retail. Global retailers, such as the well-known leading multi-brand retailers Farftech, YNAP, Mytheresa, or Luisa Via Roma (Guercini & Runfola, 2015; Guercini et al., 2020a), have emerged as leading online players. These retailers represent luxury destinations for many clients. The digital world has also generated a series of initiatives linked to sustainability issues. For example, e-commerce platforms offer second-hand or vintage products (Ryding et al., 2018), both through forms of collaborative consumption and through new e-commerce players, such as the well-known brand Rent the Runaway (Pantano & Stylos, 2020). This phenomenon seems to have an increasingly marked spread given consumers' appreciation toward circular economy issues, and should grow with estimated rates of 10% by 2023 (Pantano & Stylos, 2020). E-commerce is a broad context in terms of business models concerning these sustainable initiatives. For example, in their study, Battle et al. (2018), discussing the accessible-consumption business model, identify four new business models in the luxury fashion industry related to this trend: "swapping", which involves the exchange of fashion products according to a barter logic; "fashion libraries", with libraries of garments from which the consumer can choose; "renting", namely the rental of clothing through dedicated platforms; "sharing", with the rental of clothes between consumers.

The e-commerce environment also includes companies' business models that offer digital native luxury fashion brands connected with the manufacturing world. We consider this as the fourth business model that seems to emerge in luxury. These new players exploit new ICT trends and opportunities to fashion (see, e.g., Noris et al., 2021). This phenomenon concerns the use of the e-commerce and other technical aspects related to the new industrial paradigm of Industry 4.0 are also combined (Runfola & Perna, 2017). New technologies, such as the Internet of Things, Artificial Intelligence, 3D printing, to name a few, have tremendous implications both in the design and production other than in the sales of luxury products. For example, within luxury shoemaking, there are cases of companies trying to implement new Industry 4.0 technologies to support business model change (see, e.g., Pascucci et al., 2020). They are also particularly appreciated by new generations of consumers such as Millennials or Generation Z. The business models are strongly oriented toward a value proposition linked to the technological dimension. They are models of a hybrid nature, which mix the digital world with the real world.

In general terms, it is a phenomenon that has given rise to models also proposed by actors already established in the luxury industry, such as MNEs. For example, Cabigiosu (2020) discusses the emergence of the "see now buy now" business model. Some big luxury players, using new technologies, offer a part of their collections immediately available after the fashion shows, revolutionizing the timing of production and sale. However, brands attributable to start-ups and new players in the luxury market also fall into this category. As highlighted by Gutsatz and Heine (2018), luxury today is "*highly entrepreneurial*" (p. 409) since it sees the rise of new entrepreneurial initiatives, also with the possibility that new technologies offer to access to a market with fewer barriers to entry than in the past.

Furthermore, starting up in a digital era may lead to the development of initiatives mixing the online channels' opportunities and sustainability. Take as an example the case of The Moiré (www.the-moire.com/), a Milan-based company. The brand's origin dates back to 2019 and regards an entrepreneurial initiative that aims to reduce fashion impacts, offering an ecological and ethical value proposition. The company sells high-end fashion items, such as bags and trench coats, that are eco-friendly as the company uses only environmentally sustainable materials, including vegan productions. Furthermore, all materials used are recyclable and reusable.[8] Besides, the brand donates part of the profits to sustain initiatives for planting trees and, in fact, it has a forest by partnering with a third player. The brand sells its products both offline and through online channels. Nevertheless, it is interesting that the company destines part of the assortment only for selling on the e-commerce website and to some exclusive online retailers, such as Luisa Via Roma.[9]

Thus, this fourth business model typology concerns also digital brands linked to manufacturing skills located in industrial districts.

Once again, the Italian context offers a series of business experiences. For example, Perna et al. (2018) propose the case of the brand DIS (www.designitalianshoes.com) created by a start-up managed by three young entrepreneurs, which sells customized luxury footwear Made in Italy through digital platforms. The brand offers the opportunity to customize shoes in millions of combinations through proprietary software by combining different models, leathers, soles, and inscriptions.[10] One of the company's strengths is the online 3D configurator (Perna et al., 2018). The company produces the shoes through agreements with suppliers specialized in Made in Italy craftsmanship and quickly ships to various international markets. Suppliers come from the Marche Region, a geographical area of Italy where there is a tradition of shoe making within a cluster of companies. Therefore, the brand originates in the digital context but is strongly connected with manufacturing as the company manages production opportunities that come from the heritage of an Italian region (Perna et al., 2018). Customization is a trend in luxury, facilitated by digital and new technologies that enable the development of new business initiatives. Moreover, the company has invested in the offline context. In fact, along with the e-commerce platform, it sells its customized

---

[8] https://www.the-moire.com/

[9] https://www.the-moire.com/trench

[10] https://www.designitalianshoes.com/en/how-it-works

shoes in more than thirty-nine selected boutiques in different locations in Italy and around the world, including stores in locations in EU countries (such as Germany, France, Spain, or Austria) and non-EU countries (such as the US, Japan, South Korea, UAE, Qatar, or Ukraine).[11] The mix of offline and online lets the company offer its customers assistance through shoe stylists on the e-commerce website and in the stores.

Similarly, there are cases from the clothing industry. An interesting case is that of Lanieri Italia (www.lanieri.com/en), a Milan-based company. Two young entrepreneurs founded Lanieri in 2013. Lanieri is an e-commerce platform that offers customized menswear through a brand, Lanieri, whose positioning is based on the exclusivity of the product and Made in Italy. The company also pays particular attention to sustainability issues as it proposes Made in Italy productions, zero waste, and fair working conditions. The company relies on an online configurator to let consumers verify the fitting and customize garments. It also offers the possibility to get in touch with style advisors through videocalls. The website offers the possibility to personalize menswear through a process that starts from selecting fabrics to personalizing the garment. Consumers can select the different designs, styles, materials, colors of the fabric.[12] Moreover, consumers can select the brands of fabrics, including primary suppliers from the Biella district. Biella is among the most refined Italian districts specialized in producing wool yarn and fabrics, with leading international players such as Ermenegildo Zegna or Reda Group being vertically integrated with garments production (Cedrola & Trabaldo Togna, 2020). After the selection of the fabric, the consumer can customize the garment. The website offers more than 10 million combinations that include various options such as buttons, linings, and pockets,[13] to cite a few. It is interesting to note that the company has also physical stores where consumers can personalize their garments. In addition, they have opened stores in Italy and some foreign markets, including Belgium, France, and Switzerland. The company's turnover reached more than 3 million euros in 2017, with

[11] https://www.designitalianshoes.com/it/negozi

[12] https://www.lanieri.com/en/how-it-works

[13] https://www.lanieri.com/en/how-it-works

roughly 50% generated by international sales.[14] In 2020, Reda Group, a leading player of the Biella district and widely recognized luxury fashion player that formerly supported the start-up, acquired Lanieri. The acquisition aimed at integrating digital competencies and omnichannel orientation within the group activities.[15]

Ultimately, although this business model, compared to the previous ones, is indeed small in terms of impact on sales in the luxury industry, it still represents a phenomenon capable of proposing new brands for the world of luxury. Furthermore, the fact that it originates on the Internet makes the digital brand potentially international from the beginning, although the Internet also has barriers to internationalization, just as the physical world (Guercini & Runfola, 2015). Figure 4.6 below shows the main features of this model. The global reach that the Internet can grant represents a potential for the development of international brand awareness. In this respect, companies may rely on developing digital competencies to target new consumers, such as new generations in different foreign markets. The fact that manufacturing is still an essential value of the offering opens new scenarios for the future. The Italian cases described in this section, for example, can lever advancements in technologies, following the new Industry 4.0 industrial revolution paradigm and heritage from industrial districts that are highly recognized worldwide for fine and quality productions. They mix technology innovation with traditional production by offering customized solutions to innovate the luxury offering. Moreover, this business model may represent a bridge between the traditional luxury production locations and foreign markets, enabled by digital technologies. In other words, new players as those described here, may represent the *trait d'union* between global luxury consumers from a variety of international markets and suppliers operating in different pipeline stages from traditional luxury markets, such as Italy.

[14] https://www.repubblica.it/economia/2018/07/21/news/l_abito_italiano_su_misura_on_line_lanieri_la_startup_di_sartoria_premiata_da_altagamma-202026643/

[15] https://www.pambianconews.com/2020/11/16/reda-rileva-il-sarto-digitale-lanieri-304776

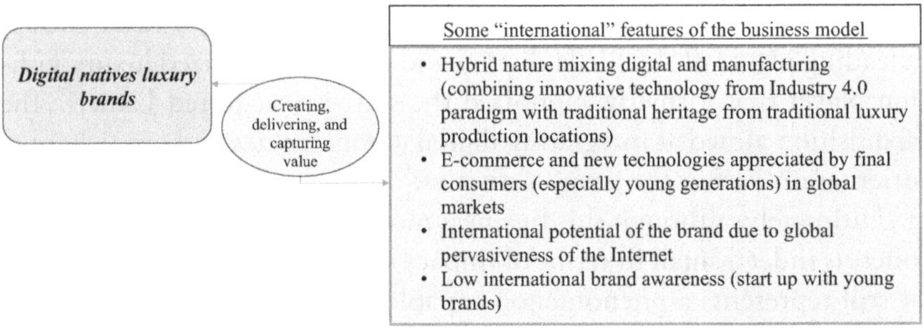

Fig. 4.6 The identity card of digital natives luxury brands. (Source: Authors' elaboration)

We finally have to point out that the digital channel and new technologies are pervasive in the current competitive environment. Traditional players and newcomers adopt them to strengthen their position in the luxury industry. Hybrid forms of business models may emerge. Hence, in the future, new initiatives could see different mixes of digital and traditional marketing tools.

4.7 Toward an International View of Business Models

To summarize, this chapter aimed to show some business models of luxury fashion companies. The chapter is not exhaustive of all the possible categories. The world of luxury is fast evolving. Trends that have already been underway for years (such as the role of sustainability and digitalization of business models) and the impact of the current pandemic scenario ask for business model evolution. In this chapter, however, we showed the variety of business models and the role of internationalization in value creation, value delivery, and value capture. In all the four models proposed, the international dimension characterizes the business model's components, fuels its growth, and represents, at the same time, a challenge to be managed. As stated in previous chapters, it relates to doing business in the luxury industry. In contrast, the literature on business models considers it a strategy within a range of implementable alternatives. We also pointed out the essential role of manufacturing activities to set up a successful luxury brand.

Our analysis seems to reveal a research gap, which proposes interesting theoretical and managerial implications. The international dimension of the business model of luxury manufacturing companies is then a promising area of research. The following chapters analyze cases of Italian luxury fashion companies and investigate the interplay between internationalization and business models.

References

Achille, A., & Zipser, D. (2020). A perspective for the luxury-goods industry during—And after—Coronavirus. *McKinsey & Company Report, 5*, 2020.

Battle, A., Ryding, D., & Henninger, C. E. (2018). Access-based consumption: A new business model for luxury and secondhand fashion business? In Ryding, D., Henninger, C.E. & Blazquez Cano, M. (Eds.), *Vintage Luxury Fashion: Exploring the Rise of Secondhand Clothing Trade* (pp. 29–44). Palgrave.

Baù, M., Block, J. H., Discua Cruz, A., & Naldi, L. (2017). Locality and internationalization of family firms. *Entrepreneurship & Regional Development, 29*, 5–6.

Cabigiosu, A. (2020). The omnichannel strategy in the fashion industry. In *Digitalization in the luxury fashion industry* (pp. 71–101). Palgrave Macmillan.

Casadesus-Masanell, R., & Ricart, J. E. (2010). From strategy to business models and onto tactics. *Long Range Planning, 43*(2–3), 195–215.

Cedrola, E., & Trabaldo Togna, L. A. (2020). Eccellenze Italiane. In *Internazionalizzazione ed ecostostenibilità del distretto tessile biellese*. Pearson.

D'Arpizio, C., & Levato, F. (2020). *Pandemic spurs a transformation of the luxury market*. Infographic: Pandemic Spurs a Transformation of the Luxury Market | Bain & Company.

D'Arpizio, C., Levato, F., Prete, F., Gault, C., & de Montgolfier, J. (2021). *The future of luxury: Bouncing back from Covid-19*. https://www.bain.com/insights/the-future-of-luxury-bouncing-back-from-covid-19/

De Marchi, V., Gereffi, G., & Grandinetti, R. (2017). Evolutionary trajectories of industrial districts in global value chains. In De Marchi, V., Di Maria, E., & Gereffi, G. (Eds.) *Local clusters in global value chains* (pp. 33–50). Routledge.

Deloitte. (2020). *Global powers of luxury goods 2020. The new age of fashion and luxury.* https://www2.deloitte.com/it/it/pages/consumer-business/articles/deloitte-global-powers-of-luxury-goods-2020%2D%2D-deloitte-italy%2D%2D-c.html. Accessed 26 Mar 2021.

Demil, B., & Lecocq, X. (2010). Business model evolution: In search of dynamic consistency. *Long Range Planning, 43*(2–3), 227–246.

Depeyre, C., Rigaud, E., & Seraidarian, F. (2018). Coopetition in the French luxury industry: Five cases of brand-building by suppliers of luxury brands. *Journal of Brand Management, 25*(5), 463–473.

Donzé, P. Y. (2018). The birth of luxury big business: LVMH, Richemont and Kering. In Donzé, P.Y., & Fujioka, R. (Eds.) *Global luxury* (pp. 19–38). Palgrave.

Doyle, S. A., & Moore, C. M. (2018). Luxury brand outsiders: Understanding the success of British and American luxury brands. In *Global luxury* (pp. 65–86). Palgrave.

Fionda, A. M., & Moore, C. M. (2009). The anatomy of the luxury fashion brand. *Journal of Brand Management, 16*(5), 347–363.

Foss, N. J., & Saebi, T. (2017). Fifteen years of research on business model innovation: How far have we come, and where should we go? *Journal of Management, 43*(1), 200–227.

Gamble, J. R., Clinton, E., & Díaz-Moriana, V. (2021). Broadening the business model construct: Exploring how family-owned SMEs co-create value with external stakeholders. *Journal of Business Research, 130*, 646–657.

Gereffi, G. (1994). The organization of buyer-driven global commodity chains: How US retailers shape overseas production networks. In G. Gereffi & M. Korzeniewicz (Eds.), *Commodity chains and global capitalism* (pp. 95–122). Greenwood Press.

Gereffi, G. (2001). Global sourcing in the US apparel industry. *Journal of Textile and Apparel, Technology and Management, 2*(1), 1–5.

Gereffi, G., Humphrey, J., & Sturgeon, T. (2005). The governance of global value chains. *Review of International Political Economy, 12*(1), 78–104.

Giacosa, E. (2014). The family business model in the luxury fashion context. In *Innovation in luxury fashion family business*. Palgrave Pivot.

Guercini, S., & Milanesi, M. (2017). Extreme luxury fashion: Business model and internationalization process. *International Marketing Review, 34*(3), 403–424.

Guercini, S., & Runfola, A. (2004). Sourcing strategies in clothing retail firms: Product complexity versus overseas supply chain. *Journal of Customer Behaviour, 3*(3), 305–334.

Guercini, S., & Runfola, A. (2010). Business networks and retail internationalization: A case analysis in the fashion industry. *Industrial Marketing Management, 39*(6), 908–916.

Guercini, S., & Runfola, A. (2011). Marketing cooperation and public policy in Italian networks of fashion firms. In Lundberg, H., & Johanson, M. (Eds.) *Network strategies for regional growth* (pp. 163–184). Palgrave Macmillan.

Guercini, S., & Runfola, A. (2015). Internationalization through e-commerce. The case of multibrand luxury retailers in the fashion industry. In *International marketing in the fast changing world*. Emerald Group Publishing Limited.

Guercini, S., & Runfola, A. (2019). Developing fashion retail operations to growth in emerging markets. *Journal of Global Fashion Marketing, 10*(2), 145–162.

Guercini, S., & Runfola, A. (2021b). Adapting business models in buyer-seller relationships: Paradoxes in the fast fashion supply chain. *Journal of Business and Industrial Marketing, 36*(8), 1273–1285.

Guercini, S., & Runfola, A. (2021a). Heuristics in decision-making by exporting textiles SMEs. *Journal of Global Fashion Marketing, 12*(1), 1–15.

Guercini, S., Milanesi, M., Mir-Bernal, P., & Runfola, A. (2020a). Surfing the waves of new marketing in luxury fashion: the case of online multi-brand retailers. In Martínez-López, F.J., & D'Alessandro, S. (Eds.) *Advances in Digital Marketing and eCommerce*, Springer Proceedings in Business and Economics.

Guercini, S., Ranfagni, S., & Runfola, A. (2020b). E-commerce internationalization for top luxury fashion brands: Some emerging strategic issues. *Journal of Management Development, 39*(4), 423–436.

Gutsatz, M. (2014). China: Incubator of luxury's new business models. In Atwal, G., & Bryson, D. (Eds.) *Luxury brands in emerging markets* (pp. 165–173). Palgrave Macmillan.

Gutsatz, M., & Heine, K. (2018). Luxury brand-building and development: New global challenges, new business models. *Journal of Brand Management, 25*(5), 409–410.

Heine, K., & Gutsatz, M. (2015). Luxury brand building in China: Eight case studies and eight lessons learned. *Journal of Brand Management, 22*(3), 229–245.

Kapferer, J. N. (2012a). Abundant rarity: The key to luxury growth. *Business Horizons, 55*(5), 453–462.

Kapferer, J.-N. (2012b, April). Why luxury should not delocalize. *The European Business Review*, pp. 58–62.

Kapferer, J.-N., & Bastien, V. (2009). *The luxury strategy*. Kogan Page Publishers.
Kashmiri, S., & Mahajan, V. (2010). What's in a name?: An analysis of the strategic behavior of family firms. *International Journal of Research in Marketing, 27*(3), 271–280.
Lechner, C., Lorenzoni, G., Guercini, S., & Gueguen, G. (2020). Supplier evolution in global value chains and the new brand game from an attention-based view. *Global Strategy Journal, 10*(3), 520–555.
Massa, L., Tucci, C. L., & Afuah, A. (2017). A critical assessment of business model research. *Academy of Management Annals, 11*(1), 73–104.
Milanesi, M., Gigliotti, M., & Runfola, A. (2020). The international marketing strategy of luxury food SMEs: The case of truffle. *Journal of Food Products Marketing, 26*(9), 600–618.
Moore, C. M., & Birtwistle, G. (2004). The Burberry business model: Creating an international luxury fashion brand. *International Journal of Retail & Distribution Management, 32*(8), 412–422.
Moore, C. M., & Doyle, S. A. (2010). The evolution of a luxury brand: The case of Prada. *International Journal of Retail and Distribution Management, 38*(11), 915–927.
Noris, A., Nobile, T. H., Kalbaska, N., & Cantoni, L. (2021). Digital fashion: A systematic literature review. A perspective on marketing and communication. *Journal of Global Fashion Marketing, 12*(1), 32–46.
Olivares-Delgado, F., Pinillos-Laffón, A., & Benlloch-Osuna, M. T. (2016). An approach to patronymic names as a resource for familiness and as a variable for family business identification. *European Journal of Family Business, 6*(1), 32–45.
Osterwalder, A., & Pigneur, Y. (2010). *Business model generation: A handbook for visionaries, game changers, and challengers*. Wiley.
Pambianconews. (2018a). *Michael Kors compra il 100% di Versace per 1,83 mld.* https://www.pambianconews.com/2018/09/25/michael-kors-compra-il-100-di-versace-per-183-mld-244337/. Accessed 26 May 2021.
Pambianconews. (2018b). *Firenze capitale della pelle.* https://www.pambianconews.com/2018/09/11/firenze-capitale-della-pelle-242756/. Accessed 26 May 2021.
Pambianconews. (2020). *Brunello Cucinelli, ricavi 2019 a 607,8 mln (+9,9%).* https://www.pambianconews.com/2020/01/07/brunello-cucinelli-ricavi-2019-a-6078-mln-99-282870/. Accessed 3 June 2021.
Pantano, E., & Stylos, N. (2020). The Cinderella moment: Exploring consumers' motivations to engage with renting as collaborative luxury consumption mode. *Psychology and Marketing, 37*(5), 740–753.

Pascucci, F., Runfola, A., Gregori, G. L., & Perna, A. (2020). *Trasformazione digitale nella filiera delle calzature di lusso. Riflessioni emergenti da un caso di studio.* Proceedings of the XVII SIM Conference, Castellanza, 29–30 ottobre 2020.

Perna, A., Runfola, A., Temperini, V., & Gregori, G. L. (2018). Problematizing customization and IT in the fashion industry: A case study of an Italian shoemaker. *Journal of Global Fashion Marketing, 9*(1), 73–86.

Ranfagni, S., & Runfola, A. (2012). Internazionalizzazione e strategie di marca. Casi d'impresa a confronto nel sistema moda italiano. *Finanza, Marketing e Produzione, 30*(2), 147–176.

Ranfagni, S., Runfola, A., & Sarti, D. (2018). International expansion based on a locally authentic brand: Issues and findings from Italian case studies. *Journal of Marketing Development & Competitiveness, 12*(1).

Ranfagni, S., Runfola, A., & Sarti, D. (2021). Family firms between territory and internationalization: An authenticity based perspective. *Entrepreneurship & Regional Development.* (In press).

Rask, M. (2014). Internationalization through business model innovation: In search of relevant design dimensions and elements. *Journal of International Entrepreneurship, 12*(2), 146–161.

Robinson, P. K., & Hsieh, L. (2016). Reshoring: A strategic renewal of luxury clothing supply chains. *Operations Management Research, 9*(3–4), 89–101.

Runfola, A., & Guercini, S. (2013). Fast fashion companies coping with internationalization: Driving the change or changing the model? *Journal of Fashion Marketing and Management, 17*(2), 190–205.

Runfola, A., & Perna, A. (2017). *Relazioni business to business e cambiamenti tecnologici: una prospettiva di marketing industriale*. FrancoAngeli.

Runfola, A., Rosati, M., & Guercini, S. (2013). New business models in online hotel distribution: Emerging private sales versus leading IDS. *Service Business, 7*(2), 183–205.

Runfola, A., Ranfagni, S., & Guercini, S. (2018). The internationalization of Italian luxury brands. The Missoni case. In Chow P., Chiu C., Yip A.C.Y., & Tang A.K.Y. (Eds.) *Contemporary case studies on fashion production, marketing and operations* (pp. 73–88). Springer.

Runfola, A., Gigliotti, M., & Picciotti, A. (2020). Modelli di business emergenti nella moda sostenibile: l'innovazione nel caso di un'organizzazione nonprofit. *Piccola Impresa/Small Business*, (3).

Runfola, A., Milanesi, M., & Guercini, S. (2021). Rethinking interaction in social distancing times: Implications for business-to-business companies. *Journal of Business and Industrial Marketing, 36*(13), 105–115.

Ryding, D., Henninger, C. E., & Cano, M. B. (Eds.). (2018). *Vintage luxury fashion: Exploring the rise of the secondhand clothing trade*. Springer.

Sarasvathy, S. D. (2001). Causation and effectuation: Toward a theoretical shift from economic inevitability to entrepreneurial contingency. *Academy of Management Review, 26*(2), 243–263.

Schneider, S., & Spieth, P. (2013). Business model innovation: Towards an integrated future research agenda. *International Journal of Innovation Management, 17*(1), 1340001.

Teece, D. J. (2010). Business models, business strategy and innovation. *Long Range Planning, 43*(2–3), 172–194.

Teece, D. J. (2018). Business models and dynamic capabilities. *Long Range Planning, 51*(1), 40–49.

Todeschini, B. V., Cortimiglia, M. N., Callegaro-de-Menezes, D., & Ghezzi, A. (2017). Innovative and sustainable business models in the fashion industry: Entrepreneurial drivers, opportunities, and challenges. *Business Horizons, 60*(6), 759–770.

Vahlne, J. E. (2020). Development of the Uppsala model of internationalization process: From internationalization to evolution. *Global Strategy Journal, 10*(2), 239–250.

Warnier, V., & Runfola, A. (2014). Guest editors' introduction: Why study business models in creative industries? *International Studies of Management & Organization, 44*(4), 3–8.

Zott, C., Amit, R., & Massa, L. (2010). The business model: Theoretical roots, recent developments, and future research. *IESE Research Papers, 3*(4), 1–43.

5

Methodology, Empirical Context, and Internationalization of Luxury Artisans

5.1 Methodology

The book employs a case study research method to address the topic under investigation. This methodology allows the analysis of a contemporary phenomenon in its context and the related dynamics. Case study research is commonly used when the units of analysis are organizations and relationships that have a complex structure and are difficult to access. Thus, the study of a single case, or a small number of cases, can provide a great deal of data, mainly qualitative (Miles & Huberman, 1994), offering insights into the nature of the phenomena. Yin (1989, p. 23) defines a case study as "an empirical inquiry that investigates a contemporary phenomenon within its real-life context when the boundaries between phenomenon and context are not evident and in which multiple sources of evidence are used". Eisenhardt (1989) highlights the potential of case studies to capture the dynamics of the phenomenon under study, maintaining that "the case study is a research strategy which focuses on understanding the dynamics present within single settings" (Eisenhardt, 1989, p. 534). In other words, case studies do not provide statistical representativeness, but they offer depth and comprehensiveness for understanding

A. Runfola et al., *Internationalization of Luxury Fashion Firms*, Palgrave Advances in Luxury, https://doi.org/10.1007/978-3-030-88755-1_5

the specific phenomenon (Easton, 1995). The aim is to achieve an in-depth understanding, not a generalization. Eisenhardt (1989) also underlines that cases can be used to generate and test a theory. The case study approach springs from at least two communication processes (Guercini, 2004a): (1) between the researcher and the organization under investigation or, more precisely, between the investigator and the subjects that represent the interface within the unit, organization, or social system under study; and (2) between the researcher and the reader or user of the research.

To the aim of the present research, a multiple-case study method is employed, which includes six cases of Italian luxury fashion companies, focusing on their business model and internationalization. The Italian fashion industry is taken as the empirical context of the study, which also benefits from the past decades of research experience held by the authors in this field. The six cases have been selected following some criteria: they are all Italian SMEs with manufacturing skills, a long tradition in the luxury fashion industry, and a process of internationalization developed over the years. In addition to these criteria, the availability/will of the entrepreneurs and managers to be involved in the research process was a relevant condition to carry on with the development of the cases. The six cases (Bontoni, Sapaf, Fabiana Filippi, Antonelli Firenze, Monnalisa, E.Marinella) cover different sectors of the luxury fashion industry, including womenswear, menswear, childrenswear, and leather goods.

Data were collected from different data sources. For four cases out of six (Bontoni, Sapaf, Fabiana Filippi, and Antonelli Firenze), interviews were the primary source of data. More specifically, in-depth, semi-structured interviews with entrepreneurs and managers were conducted over the last three years. To ensure triangulation and the robustness of data (Eisenhardt, 1989; Barrat et al., 2011), data were collected from secondary sources, including company website and annual reports (last 5 years), internal reports provided by the companies, fashion magazines, previously published interviews and videos. The cases of Monnalisa and E.Marinella were based exclusively on secondary data.

As for the case analysis, a first step concerned a within-case analysis to develop the individual case by performing content analysis of documents from the secondary sources and transcripts of the interviews. Such data were then systematized to develop a clear picture of the business model of each company and a full chronology of the internationalization process. The within-case analysis resulted in the six cases. Two of them are presented in the next sections, and the other four in the next chapter. A cross-case analysis was then employed to identify and discuss similarities and differences between the cases through a pattern-matching technique (Miles & Huberman, 1994) that allowed the identification of common themes related to the business model of luxury fashion SMEs and their expansion in foreign markets. In the next section, the empirical context of the study, namely the Italian fashion industry, is presented, followed by a focus on the leather industry and the two cases of the leather companies.

5.2 The Empirical Context of the Study

The Italian fashion industry occupies a frontline position in the world for international competitiveness, defending its international leadership both in the textile-clothing and in the leather/footwear sectors. There are antecedents for this in the role of the country in the Western culture, but the contemporary industry success began to take shape in the early 1950s. Historians trace the first concrete step toward the fashion industry that is now internationally recognized to February 12, 1951, the day on which the Marquis Gian Battista Giorgini organized the first Italian fashion show in Florence. Only a small group of people was invited to the show, including some important foreign buyers and fashion journalists, who showed great interest in the talent and skill of Italian designers. Driven by this success, the Italian tailors started to sell their creations in the international markets, entering into direct competition with the French fashion, which, until the 1950s, held the absolute dominance of the sector.

Subsequently, in the 1960s, Italian *haute-couture* and made-to-measure clothes were joined by *prêt-à-porter*, with ready-made clothes at lower prices. The intuition of going beyond the *haute-couture* toward an industrial product with a strong stylistic connotation opened up a phase of strong development in the sector. With this new approach, which became a common factor in all fashion productions (clothing, leather goods, and footwear) during the same period, between the end of the 1970s and the 1980s, the Italian *prêt-à-porter* managed to compete successfully at an international level (Settembrini, 1994). These are the years in which the phenomenon of fashion brands exploded, which still guarantee Made in Italy a solid international reputation.

Under the thrust of the great driving force of the positive experience of Italian *prêt-à-porter*, a productive context developed. It showed a strong ability to industrialize the creative content through a network of companies that oversees the entire manufacturing process, both in the textile/clothing sector and in that of leather goods and footwear. This ability to combine the creative dimension with a particularly reactive industrial component is the key element of the development of Made in Italy in those years. The organization model of the industrial production chain, for example, in textile and clothing (Jones, 2002), in particular the industrial district model (Aage & Belussi, 2008), also played a fundamental role in this integration process (Paris, 2010).

Therefore, the Italian fashion industry was—and still is—organized in an archipelago of specialized territorial areas made of SMEs that benefit from a condition of geographical proximity as an opportunity for contamination and knowledge (Lazzeretti & Capone, 2016). In that period, and up to the mid-1990s, the use of this model of territorial agglomeration represented a unique means of transformation of creative processes into opportunities for industrial development, generating wealth and employment. Examples are the historic textile districts of Prato and Biella, the leather goods district in the province of Florence, or the footwear district in the Marche region (Guercini, 2004b). Alongside the supply chain and the organization in industrial districts, another key factor in the development of the Italian fashion industry has been the construction of virtuous alliances with mechanical, electronic, and chemical companies, which have made an essential contribution to the innovation processes.

The history of the Italian fashion industry is the history of a continuous ability to interpret and adapt to market changes. In the last decade, the advance of competition from developing countries that benefit from a strong advantage on labor costs, the technological acceleration in the field of chemistry, textile machinery, electronics, as well as the emergence of new consumer opportunities, have imposed a radical change of the typical traits of the Italian fashion industry (Sammarra & Belussi, 2006). In this new context, the industry, to defend its international leadership, has redefined its structure by introducing at least two important paths of change on a strategic-organizational level. In the first place, under the pressure of globalization and the competitive advantages expressed by the newly industrialized countries, relations between companies have tended to go beyond consolidated national borders to access international production networks, thus modifying the traditional district model. Secondly, the widening of the boundaries of competition beyond the area of advanced countries has forced companies to give up basic production and accelerate investments in medium to high-end products. This repositioning is redesigning the fashion supply chain in the direction of a hybrid system in which there is an increasing role both of the technology-bearing sectors (mechanical, electronic, chemical, and information technology industries), and a complex system of services (styling, marketing, retailing) bearer of intangible product content (Berger, 2005; Merlo, 2018). These changes have affected the industry globally, but for companies in Italy it has meant less than in other countries a disappearance of manufacturing activity, thanks also to the margins obtained due to the repositioning in the luxury field and in some cases to vertical integration in distribution by manufacturing businesses (Guercini, 2004b).

It should be noted immediately that the ongoing process of strategic repositioning in the direction of product ranges with greater added value and, therefore, with greater technological and styling value requires a more extensive concept of the fashion supply chain. The supply chain is the only interpretation that allows a representation of the actual articulation of production activities and services, through which the integrated process that generates the final value of the product is achieved.

The push of the sector toward growing attention to the intangible contents of the fashion product, the growing operational integration with distribution, commercial and industrial expansion toward foreign markets, and a general need to improve quality standards and the technological content of processes and products are elements that have generated a growing need of the fashion company to integrate more and more with a specialized supply chain, both in the field of intangible services and in the field of process and product technologies (Carmignani, 2016). Based on these assumptions, the fashion system becomes that set of companies that compete with their activities not only in the cycle of industrial transformation but also in that of technological and immaterial enhancement. Characterizing element of this system is the international vocation, a trait present since the dawn of the Italian fashion industry (Guercini, 2004b) and evidenced by the data.

Before the arrival of the COVID-19 pandemic, the export of Italian fashion was registering a growing trend, with a value of 42 billion euros in the first nine months of 2019, +6% compared to the previous year (elaboration on ISTAT—"Istituto Nazionale di Statistica", the Italian National Institute of Statistics—data). In particular, the increase concerned exports of clothing (+7.6%) which exceeded 14 billion euros, bags (+12.8%) with 9.5 billion euros, footwear (+5.4%) with around 8 billion euros, and knitwear (+6.3%) with 2.7 billion euros. The major Italian exporters are the province of Florence for footwear and leather goods (with a rapid growth of 55.1% in one year), Milan for clothing (+7%). Lombardy was the first Italian region in 2019 with 10.4 billion euros of exports, representing a quarter of the Italian total (+3.5%). Tuscany also exceeded 10 billion euros (+26%).

The important growth recorded in Tuscany in terms of exports is mainly attributable to the leather goods sector, with the main Italian district in the province of Florence. More generally, the Italian leather goods sector closed in 2019 with decidedly positive results, driven once again by exports (+58% in value in the three years 2016–2019). Foreign sales of leather goods reached new records in value, with a consequent significant consolidation of the trade balance (+39%), against a slight decline in the domestic market. According to the findings of Confindustria Moda for

Assopellettieri, in the first ten months of the year, exports grew by 25.8% in value over the same period of 2018 (almost 8.6 billion euros), with a decidedly contained increase, however, in terms of volume (+0.8%) and a surge in average prices (+24.7%). The main countries of destination for leather goods exports are Switzerland, the most important logistics-distribution platform of the main fashion/luxury fashion brands, which recorded a doubling in value (+102.6%), France, also linked in part to outsourcing of the large global players, which overtook Germany, and the United States in the third position. There was also a favorable trend recorded on the Asian markets: in addition to South Korea and Japan, there are also Taiwan and Thailand, two countries considered to be investment destinations in the immediate future.

The positive trend of the sector, however, hides some critical issues. The final figures for 2019 confirm that the sector runs substantially at "two speeds": very fast as regards the big global brands, such as Gucci, Prada, or Ferragamo, while SMEs with their brand struggle more. The entrepreneurial fabric of Italian leather goods is made up of a large number of very small companies (70% have no more than five employees), for many of which the year has reserved results far from the general ones, and 2020 was definitively fatal. In general, the pandemic crisis has put a strain on the leather goods sector. The data processed by the Confindustria Moda for Assopellettieri show strongly penalizing trends for all the main variables, with a drastic reduction in turnover in the second quarter (-49.2%, with decreases of more than 50% for six out of ten companies in the sample analyzed), which follows -37.1% in the first part of the year.

Expectations, however, concern a strong positive rebound, driven again by exports and the primary role of industrial districts, one above all that of Tuscany. In the area of the province of Florence, from Scandicci, Lastra a Signa and Impruneta to, in the south, Pontassieve and the Val di Sieve, there is the Florentine pole of leather goods, a luxury district whose production is mainly represented by leather goods such as bags, wallets, and small leather goods, belts and other items such as luggage and business bags, which can be placed in the high price/quality range (up to the luxury segment) or medium-high. In addition to this type of production, there are also companies specialized in the footwear sector. The leather goods district undoubtedly benefits from its proximity to the tanning district of S. Croce sull'Arno, located in central Tuscany, which extends over a radius of 10 kilometers and represents one of the main realities in the field of tanning processing at an Italian and international level (Dei Ottati, 2004).

Large Italian brands (to name a few, Gucci, Ferragamo, Prada, Valentino, etc.) and foreign ones coexist on the Florentine territory. Foreign brands have chosen the district as the location of their operating units (e.g., Balenciaga, Yves Saint Laurent, and Dior). There are also SMEs with their brands, characterized by a distinct artisan vocation, often custodians of indispensable know-how. The leading companies that sell their brand on the final market make use of a network of suppliers and sub-suppliers—the SMEs—to whom they delegate most of the phases of the production process, internalizing the phases considered to be the most strategic (product development, engineering, cutting) (Milanesi et al., 2020).

In the area, there is, therefore, a constellation of SMEs located in the different production phases of the leather supply chain, which are part of the supply network of the final companies as first- or second-level suppliers. Such firms specialize in a specific process or manufacturing stages and often work entirely for a single brand. In most cases, they do not oversee strategic phases such as product conception but have production skills that make them strategic partners for leading companies by providing technical support in phases such as product development and engineering. However, there is no lack of virtuous cases of SMEs that have developed their brand over time, mainly targeting foreign markets while maintaining, in most cases, the role of suppliers for the global players of luxury.

Even if Tuscany hosts the first district for Italian leather goods, there are also other relevant cases. The Marche footwear district has its nerve center in Sant'Elpidio a Mare, in the heart of the Marche region. Home to the production of shoes of famous brands, this district represents the Made in Italy in the world as regards the handcrafted footwear. The district, thanks to its territory rich in waterways for tanning, herds, and flocks for leather, processes the raw materials directly on-site and entrusts the processing of the various parts of the footwear to third-party companies. This is how specialized companies, such as heel and upper factories, started to work in the district, and nowadays, they are an integral part of this complex process and contribute to the quality of the finished product, characterized by a unique and highly recognizable style (Cutrini, 2011).

Two cases of companies operating in the leather goods sector are therefore proposed: Sapaf, a historic company in the Florentine territory for the production of luxury bags, both on behalf of third parties and with its brand, and Bontoni, a handcrafted shoemaker that creates and produces luxury male shoes, located in the Marche district. The two companies not only share their belonging to the leather goods sector but are both presented as emblematic cases of small-sized companies with a vocation for internationalization since their origins.

5.3 The Case of Sapaf: International Vocation and Networking for Innovation in the "art" of Leather Goods[1]

5.3.1 The Origin of the Firm and Its Profile

Founded in 1954 in Florence, Sapaf, a name that stands for Società Artigiana Pelletterie Artistiche Fiorentine, is a small company with positive competitive and turnover performance and a solid orientation to international markets since its origins. The 2019 financial statements indicate a turnover up by about 60% compared to just five years earlier. In the same year, the net profit was approximately 10% of turnover. The

[1] The case is written by Simone Guercini. The case is based on secondary data and information gathered by means of interviews and meetings with the CEO of the company Andrea Calistri. The author also visited the company and participated to sector events. We thank Andrea Calistri for kind availability and for sharing information about the company.

company turnover has been strongly growing in recent years: equal to about 1.1 million euros in 2014, it reached about 1.8 million in 2019, then marking a decline in 2020 concerning the effects of the pandemic on luxury consumption, amounting to around 1.2 million.

The foreign markets, mainly in the European Union in the years from 2014 to 2018, were predominantly non-European in 2019 and 2020. Throughout this period, purchases by domestic customers remained lower than 10% of the total turnover.

Sapaf is a family business run by the offspring of the founders. It produces luxury leather goods, in particular bags, which represented almost 90% of the value of sales in 2019. The company is a supplier of major luxury fashion brands and designers for these products, focusing its expertise on the design and manufacture of bags and other leather goods, but it also has its brand. It is interesting to note how the company is representative of a system of SMEs that are part of the leather district in the Florentine area. As already mentioned, this part of Italy represents an essential context for the production of leather accessories and other luxury products. Some international luxury brands (e.g., Gucci and Ferragamo) have headquarters and most others have subsidiaries. Most international luxury brands have a direct (with the head office or their organizational units) or indirect presence (mainly through buyers and agents) in Florence or the surrounding area.

Sapaf locates in Scandicci, near Florence, where it moved more than forty years ago after starting its activities in the city center. The company's full name (Società Artigiana Pelletterie Artistiche Fiorentine) highlights an approach to the activities and the product (artistic dimension) dating back to the Florentine tradition in the leather goods sector.

The history of the company, with the stages of its development, is characterized by the role of the internationalization process. On the one hand, foreign markets have always shown an interest in Florentine leather goods, of which Sapaf is an expression. On the other hand, the company has always been proactive and dynamic in its relationship with the domestic and foreign markets through collaboration with other companies in the same sector and territory. Despite its small size, the company has specific visibility and has achieved success in recent years, as evidenced by the commercial results (as mentioned, there was an increase in turnover of about 60% in five years, from 2014 to 2019) and positive economic results.

5.3.2 The Product, the Target, and the Main Trends

The company operates in the luxury market, mainly producing bags as a supplier of international luxury fashion brands. In the words of Andrea Calistri, Chief Executive Officer (CEO), member of the second entrepreneurial generation, and with a critical leading role in the company, the target of Sapaf is a "*woman who belongs to a high-spending class, who can spend thousand euros for a bag*". Sapaf works mainly as a supplier, but the company also has its brand (Sapaf 54 Atelier) sold in multi-brand stores and the Sapaf digital store. Sapaf recently updated the digital store.

Some significant trends that have changed the scenario in recent years have also affected the company. The first significant change concerns the trading processes, with the progressive transition from a long supply chain, made up of four steps (two levels of subcontracting, the luxury brand, and the retail), to a more and more direct chain, which meant getting closer to the end customer. A second change concerns digital technologies. Even in the luxury leather goods sector, the recent pandemic has accelerated the adoption of digital technologies to keep relationships with customers, affecting both the B2B and B2C. In 2020, Sapaf inaugurated a digital store translated into English and Italian to sell the Sapaf 54 Atelier products. The digitalization of the relationship with the market was preceded by introducing a customer relationship management system for managing both B2B and B2C to consumer relationships.

The adoption of digital technologies by the company also concerns manufacturing activities. Sapaf shows a general propensity to invest in technology and training, which is not always present with equal intensity in companies in the same sector, often with a position of entrepreneurial leadership compared to all the companies of the same sector and size in the same territory.

The history of Sapaf is marked by the evolution of the international scenario in which the development of Florentine leather goods is generated. Sapaf was founded in the 1950s in the context of development following the Marshall Plan and growth in international demand. In those same years, a development cycle of the Italian fashion industry began, which has a primary driving force in Florence. The CEO recalls how "*Giovan Battista Giorgini was the one who coined the idea of Made in Italy, with the first fashion show in his villa in 1951, followed by the famous fashion shows in the White Room of Palazzo Pitti*".

A characteristic of the company is having top management connected to the network of artisan leather goods companies that operate in Florence and the surrounding area. The CEO Andrea Calistri has held essential roles in the leather goods trade associations and has been president of a consortium, Centopercento Italiano, which is an essential player in the development of marketing experiences also at an international level for a large group of Italian leather goods companies, mainly the Florentine ones (Guercini & Woodside, 2012). Centopercento Italiano is a consortium created by leather goods companies with the participation of related actors (including a local bank) to support the initiatives of companies committed to maintaining their production in Italy—in a historical phase characterized by a strong push toward relocation in emerging countries—with high standards of quality, and environmental and social sustainability. The consortium supported advanced ecological certification processes on this front already about two decades ago, subsequently continuing its commitment to supporting the initiatives of companies toward the creation of access channels to the consumer market. Another feature of the company, connected in part to the previous one, is the participation in initiatives for the training and transmission of skills in the sector.

The company also develops its international activities through cooperation with other companies in the sector and the area. The two dimensions are partly overlapping, considering that the Florentine area is the one with the highest concentration of companies in the sector at the Italian level. Andrea Calistri is a member of sectoral (AIMPES MIPEL), and territorial associations (CNA Florence). Mipel is the leading international leather goods fair, held twice a year in Milan, and in 2020 it switched to a digital format as a response to the challenge of the pandemic. In the 1980s, the company also began to be visible in the press dedicated to the sector, with photos of its products appearing in magazines such as *Women's Wear Daily, Vogue, Mipel Magazine, ARS Arpel.*

Sapaf maintains constant attention to the use of new technologies applied to leather goods, starting with developing models and production. This attention is concretized in a commitment on the training front, experienced personally by the top management through participation in courses and the support for training initiatives in the design and manufacturing of leather goods. On the subject of innovation training, the company showed sensitivity early on. For example, as early as 1986, Andrea Calistri held a course at CFP San Colombano on the possibilities of using computers to develop models in collaboration with Redwall of Pianoro (Bologna).

In the 2000s, with the Italian Centopercento Consortium, the I-Place format was born, followed in 2006 by an I-Place outlet experience intended not only for B2B as a showroom but also for B2C as a store, managed by the consortium and in which some dozen consortium companies participate. Through this experience, the company matures skills in direct sales to the consumer of its products, supporting this effort in aggregation with other companies. The company developed various promotional initiatives (collaborations at Mipel in Milan with the Ferragamo and Gucci Museum, training initiatives, studies on times and methods). In the field of training, the High School of Italian Leather Goods was born in 2005.

Since 2003, with the Italian Centopercento Consortium, SA 8000 and ISO 9001 certifications have been achieved. Subsequently, in 2008, the "Trasp-Tracce sulla pelle" project was created, dedicated to the issue of product traceability. Again, with the Italian Centopercento consortium, Sapaf participated in innovation projects concerning sustainable products and processes. The Zero Impact project started in 2011, aimed at studying innovative technical solutions for the recovery and reuse of waste and scraps from leather goods. This commitment on the technology front often takes on a purpose consistent with the objective of sustainability. Both the company and the entrepreneur Andrea Calistri are at the forefront of this issue.

Sapaf maintains a cutting-edge profile in the development and testing of technologies applied to the production of leather goods, with the experimentation of computerized cutting. Still, on the technology front, the company firmly pushes on new forms of digital communication, functional to work together with B2B partners. This experience proved to be fundamental in the recent pandemic, as—perhaps more than in other sectors—the work done together with business customers for contact, development, and communication of the work results together can be effective through new communication technologies and social media.

5.3.3 The Evolution of the International Dimension of the Business Model

In the history of the company, the term "born global" appears appropriate. Since the mid-1950s, the company has always had a vocation toward foreign markets. Most of the export regarded some major international markets, such as the United States. If we look at the proportions of this international dimension concerning the size of the company, we go well beyond the parameters defined in the literature for the "born global" company, including the achievement of at least 30% of the turnover in exports within the first two years since the foundation. We could define Sapaf as a "*born global ante litteram*", which began exporting to North America as early as 1955 (the year following its foundation), quickly allocating a considerable share of its turnover to foreign markets and looking at the international context as a reference market.

Thus, internationalization does not take place after a previous domestic development process but starts with the company's founding. The first export invoice, still preserved in the company archives, dates back to 1955 and concerns an order by a US customer sent to Puerto Rico. This continuous connection with the international dimension is found in particular in the commercial projection of the company. The company participated in the Florence Trade Fair in the 1960s, affirming its presence as an exporter in two main markets: the United States and Japan. Sapaf went through difficult times in its history. One of these was a consequence of the 1966 flood in Florence, during which it managed to rise also thanks to a fund created by Florentine fashion personalities with the involvement of large American department stores; of the 300 companies benefiting from these funds, Sapaf is one of the few still existing today. This fact also testifies to the importance that the international dimension has always had in the history of the company, a dimension that has allowed it to overcome difficult times and has guaranteed its survival and development.

In the 1970s, the relationship with international markets evolved, with Hong Kong and France becoming two relevant foreign markets in addition to the United States and Japan. The participation in the Florence Trade Fair also continued in this decade. The 1980s saw a surge in exports, favored by the competitive devaluations of the lira, but also certainly possible due to the interest shown by the international markets for the handcrafted leather goods made by the company. This growth of international markets is manifested in terms of volumes and the variety of markets, which expanded in number. A crucial element of internationalization, which from then on would have strongly characterized the company's international presence, is the collaboration with leading international luxury fashion brands, such as Celine, Gucci, Tod's, Fendi, and D&G. The increasing international presence is also represented by the number and variety of locations of the trade fairs in which the company takes part, such as Mipel in Milan, the Promopel fair in Japan, the Leather Goods from Italy fair in New York. The exporting countries have progressively grown in number and, overall, importance on turnover. In the 1990s, these markets were: United States, Japan, Hong Kong, Taiwan, Singapore, France, England, and Australia.

The company's commitment to international markets is characterized by some constants, such as the entry strategy based on exports, from indirect to mainly direct over the years, the use of fairs as an opportunity for building and maintaining contacts with customers. In the company's history, the most important foreign markets have not been the closest ones, but markets from other continents, particularly the United States and Japan. The larger European markets are undoubtedly relevant but not to the same extent. Large American department stores are the customer category that remained dominant in the company's international clientele until the end of the 1970s. From that stage onward, the Japanese market acquired increasing importance, with a significant boost during the 1980s, until the first half of the 1990s. In the words of Andrea Calistri, "from the late seventies to 1992 Japan was the most relevant international market in driving the company exports. After 1992, Japanese luxury consumption came to a halt, and we entered a phase, that of globalization."

With the globalization of the 1990s and 2000s, products started to travel from the periphery to advanced countries. Factories closed their plants in Europe or America to open new plants or to work with suppliers in East and South Asia with low labor costs.

Sapaf did not take part in this process, recognizing manufacturing skills and roots in its territory of origin as an element of its identity and its strategy. This choice is an essential part of the company's international status, which still today reaffirms this link with the Florentine territory and a continuum between tradition and constant attention to the evolutionary trends.

In the 2000s, globalization became a consolidated reality, but the markets changed face with the arrival of the euro and the development of emerging markets, mainly China, as a consumer market for luxury products and leather goods. The market sees the development of private labels.

Fairs also remained a fundamental element of internationalization, with new relevant fairs, such as the OBUV Moscow. In parallel, exports remained strong in the United States and Japan, Russia and the United Arab Emirates, and other European markets such as France and England.

5.3.4 The Relationship Between Company Profile and Internationalization Processes

The company business plan shows that the company's clientele has been almost entirely foreign for years, spreading over many markets, from the United States to the major European countries (Great Britain, Germany, France) and Asia (China and Japan). In addition, the customer portfolio appears to be more and more fragmented over the years. Customers are both small emerging designers looking for a highly experienced and reliable partner to realize their creations and international luxury fashion brands. The result is a strong diversification and, therefore, a reduction of the crisis risk of individual customers.

The internationalization process started in the 1950s and 1960s, largely through the role of the buying offices that connected the demand of big international buyers with the company's production capacities. The company's internationalization strategy has always been based on the export of products made in the country (and city) of origin, but the entry channel has evolved over the years. From the forms of indirect export through the buying office, the company moved on to an indirect channel linked to the production of private labels and the direct channel created in a business-to-business context through participation in trade fairs. Moreover, it moved on with forms of cooperation through consortia with companies in the same sector and the same territory. Despite being small in size, the company has a leadership recognized in the context of companies in the same sector and territory, pursuing internationalization strategies that rely on collaboration with other similar companies by sector, territory, and size. For example, with these other companies through the Centopercento Italiano consortium, certifications have been achieved that have supported competitiveness in the international arena.

Internationalization is effectively pursued because the company is at the forefront in responding to issues, such as sustainability, strongly perceived in the global market in which it operates, for example, by its private label customers. Sustainability is developed in multiple directions: social sustainability and responsibility toward the community; ecological responsibility and compliance with environmental protection rules (as evidenced by the certifications obtained); eco-friendly packaging solutions; duration of the products and the possibility to repair them. The top management sees limits in pursuing these ambitious objectives in the size of the individual company. It is effectively active in developing collective responses at the level of aggregates of companies with similar problems, offering pre-competitive solutions, such as the experience of the Italian Centopercento Consortium.

The company is also committed to supporting changes and challenges arising from digitalization, which also has substantial implications for the company's internationalization. The digital store is strongly connected with the international profile of the company: it is translated in English and Italian; it has been developed with foreign partners, especially German ones; the development of a sustainability strategy that starts from the evaluation of how this is understood in different cultures, for example in South Korea, even before the territory of the country of origin.

In summary, some characteristic features of the company are the followings (see Fig. 5.1):

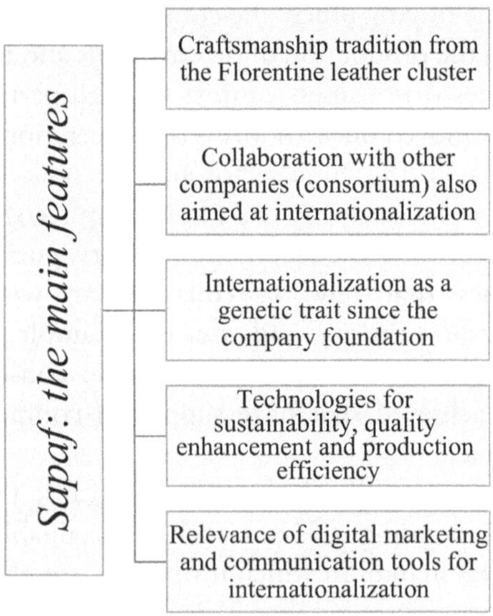

Fig. 5.1 Sapaf in pills: the main features emerging from the case. (Source: Authors' elaboration)

- The company remains consistent with its identity as an artisan company producing high-quality bags and leather goods, with manufacturing activities located in the Florentine territory.
- To keep this profile, the company has always had a dynamic and proactive approach, with collaboration strategies with other companies in the same sector and often in the same area, as evidenced by the experience of the Italian Centopercento consortium.
- The entrepreneur's personality plays a particular role in the policies of the individual company and the policies defined and pursued collectively by an influential group of Florentine leather goods companies.
- The company is committed to developing technologies for sustainability and enhancing quality and production efficiency, both individually and through the Centopercento Italiano consortium.
- Internationalization is a genetic trait of the company, the development of which cannot be separated from the projection toward international markets; the company began exporting in its first months of life, and exports consistently represent the clear majority component of the turnover;
- Digital marketing tools and digital communication tools are fundamental for the internationalization of the company.

5.4 Bontoni: Manufacturing Excellence in the Luxury Shoemaking[2]

5.4.1 The Origin of the Brand

Bontoni is a Made in Italy luxury company that produces men's shoes entirely handmade in the company laboratory. The company is located in the footwear district of Montegranaro, one of the most important Italian districts recognized worldwide for the production of men's footwear. Montegranaro is a small medieval village in the Marche region but the

[2] The case is written by Andrea Runfola. The case is based on secondary data and information gathered by means of interviews with the Founder Franco Gazzani. We thank Franco Gazzani for kind availability and for sharing information about the company.

custodian of excellent footwear knowledge and traditions. Bontoni represents a notable example of the ability to know how to enhance and maintain these traditions settled over time and develop a brand that has a strong international vocation since its inception.

It is interesting to retrace some evolutionary stages in the history of Bontoni. The brand was created in 2004. However, the company draws its origins from a business experience of over seventy years and is connected to a family firmly anchored to the footwear traditions of Montegranaro. Currently managed by the third family generation, the brand bases its roots on the passion for shoes, the ability to listen to the customer, and the manufacturing skills of an entire family of artisans.

The culture of manufacturing men's footwear has characterized it since the first generation of the family. The grandfather of the current owner was one of the first artisans of Montegranaro, a master shoemaker. At the end of the 1940s of the last century, he already produced custom-made shoes for local people and traders. The father and uncle of the current top owner also continued the path taken by the first generation, both by making custom-made shoes and working as pattern makers for many local shoe factories. Therefore, the generations before the current one represent a solid basis for the company by developing comprehensive know-how and a strong specialization in men's footwear. The third generation, therefore, bases its skills on a path of over seventy years of craftsmanship.

However, in 2004, the current top management decided to bring the Bontoni brand to the market. Bontoni was born from the will of two cousins, one located in Montegranaro and the other in the United States, to propose a collection of ready-made shoes that would complement the tradition of custom-made shoes. Therefore, the Bontoni brand from its launch is made in Italy with high-quality production and raw materials, with an artisanal characterization and completely handmade in the company workshop. The company immediately destined its proposal to international markets, representing the totality of its sales, with the American market representing the primary foreign market. Bontoni is a peculiar player in the luxury men's footwear market since it offers a tailor-made product that leverages the traditional craftsmanship of Montegranaro and strong family production skills. To date, it represents an organizational reality with a turnover that places it on the levels of a small business (about 2 million euros), but with a brand widely recognized in the specific business area of luxury men's footwear.

Although in 2020 the company moved to a new location due to space requirements, again in Montegranaro, the company's productions are still carried out in-house, given that Bontoni is an example of a "casa e bottega", namely in-house laboratory. The workshop is located in the family home since the first generation of business. The artisanal nature of the products results from a tradition linked to the work of the "shoemaker". Therefore, the company has always been an expression of it. It is an important aspect, which makes the concept of product customization absolute customization, from the conception of the model to creating the shoe and in all phases, even the most micro, that characterize the production process.

In this sense, one of the fundamental assets of the brand is the family. However, it is a concept of an extended family, which includes both the third entrepreneurial generation, which launched the Bontoni brand and previous generations and the entrepreneur's own family (his wife owns a footwear company in the district). The concept of the family comes to include employees as well. The family permeates the business offer and is considered a fundamental asset for the business model's success. It is part of the footwear heritage of the Montegranaro district and leverages this to fuel the corporate value proposition.

5.4.2 The Value Proposition: Collections and Production

Skills and product knowledge are another element at the base of the company business model. The company's manufacturing expertise allows the creation of shoe models with levels of quality standards of excellence. Bontoni offers two types of products on the market: make-to-order products, with complete customization of the shoe based on the needs and requests of the customer; ready-made products, that is, the production of footwear collections according to the styles proposed by the company. However, given that the brand can satisfy customization requests from customers, even in footwear based on the styles proposed by the company, the customer still can proceed with adaptations and customizations. The company offers the possibility to choose from many options in terms of shoe styles, materials to be used, and construction methods of the shoe and soles. The product is a formal and semi-formal classic product, which, however, is characterized by high levels of innovation combined with the maintenance of traditions and styles typical of made-in Italy footwear.

The shoes combine quality and high levels of comfort. As the company highlights, Bontoni shoes have become famous for "richly hued, hand-dyed leathers, unique lasts and meticulously hand-sew stitching" (source: company website). The production is about 40% make-to-order and 60% ready-made. Make-to-order productions represent a high percentage compared to other players in the market. It is necessary to consider that every pair of shoes is an ad hoc project, which requires investments of time, adaptations, and attention to the individual details requested by the customer. In hindsight, these are specificities that make the company's productions unique and that the company manages by leveraging the skills developed for generations. The company proceeds with seasonal orders for ready-made collections, which follow the traditional spring/summer and autumn/winter collections. The pricing is in line with a high-end positioning and varies according to the type of production.

As anticipated, the production of shoes is entirely handmade in all phases of the production process. In addition, the company's ability to respond to customer needs implies attention to detail and attention to craft resulting from a deep knowledge of shoe manufacturing. Currently, the production workshop involves about ten people (including the owner). The fact that the owner deals with both the commercial dimension and the product dimension is another peculiar element of the business model. The laboratory carries out each phase of the production process by hand, effectively making each pair of shoes a unique piece.

In addition, the excellence of the company's production relates to the ability to select the best raw materials and their wise use in the production process. The company procures its raw materials from prestigious Italian tanneries, although it also purchases from suppliers located in France and England for some types of valuable raw materials.

Given the exclusive nature of the production and the levels of customization offered, the company offers a limited production of shoes during the year (about 2100 pairs of shoes). In fact, both for the size of the company and for the time required for the production of the shoes, production times may vary and take months (about three months) necessary to follow the process of creating the new shoe with extreme detail and by hand. In addition, of course, times depend on the type of collection so that production times can be longer for products with higher levels of customization.

It is also interesting to note how the laboratory represents the protection of local knowledge. The brand has managed over time to include young staff in the productions, providing its essential contribution in maintaining the district traditions of Montegranaro. Bontoni succeeds through his work to keep alive the tradition of "handmade" at the local level.

5.4.3 The International Dimension of the Business Model

As already mentioned, the Bontoni brand has been targeting international markets since its launch.

The company is now present in some foreign markets, including the US, which, as already mentioned, represents the primary market, some European markets, and Russia. In addition, considering the ability to produce single pairs of shoes for specific consumers, the company also has customers in other foreign markets, such as Hong Kong or Dubai.

The company directly manages international markets and sells its products through the wholesale channel. It is currently present in about twenty of the most exclusive retail stores in the world. In some of these, the brand's presence is thought a shop in shop strategy. The company presents its collections in a Bontoni store within a luxury hotel chain only for the Russian market. In this case, a local partner manages the store.

The first international target market was the American market. As already mentioned, one of the two cousins who participated in the launch of the Bontoni brand is American. Hence, the brand decided to approach this market as the first foreign destination. The current top management managed, during the launch years, to obtain orders first from an exclusive store in Boston and, from there, subsequently, in other prestigious stores in the US.

One of the pillars of the brand's foreign development is Bontoni's ability to be close to customers, both distributors and final consumers. To this end, the company's top management is often physically present within the stores of its distributors. This choice is considered essential both to support the presence of the in-store brand and to acquire knowledge and interact with the end customer. Knowing how to interpret customer needs is one of the founding elements of the business model. In fact, from this comes the possibility of adaptation and the offer of full customization to requests. Being present for several days at the points of sale also allows Bontoni to carry out field tests and receive customer reactions to the various company proposals. It is also a way to understand needs and new ideas for the development of future collections. This is an activity considered central to offer a product that satisfies customers, considering the difficulties inherent in producing a customized shoe. The company can effectively manage these dimensions, given that concerning individual customers, it can know their preferences, needs, style requirements, translating them into elements of shoe design and production.

In addition to the presence in the points of sale, mode of presence abroad, which is part of the company's commercial activities, trunk shows[3] are another essential tool for development in foreign markets. In these events, which last few days, the different brands can present their collections and collect orders. In the case of Bontoni, the trunk shows allow both to collect orders for ready-made collections and individual pairs of made-to-measure shoes. Also, thanks to this moment of interaction with customers and retailers, the brand develops in-depth knowledge of the market's needs, allowing customization of shoe sizes and the most suitable materials for individual customers for a comfortable fit. Another advantage of trunk shows is the possibility of obtaining a concentration of potential contacts in a few days.

[3] A trunk show is a special event in which luxury fashion brands can show their collections directly to a selected number of customers and store sales personnel. The trunk show is hosted in retail stores or other exclusive locations.

Trunk shows and the direct presence of top management in retail stores at certain times during the year also allow for the connection with the sales associates of the stores. Sales associates are essential in the relationship between the brand and the final consumer.

Ultimately, this development approach abroad allows the top management to develop an incredible cultural background in terms of customer knowledge and the establishment of relevant relationships. As an output of this, the brand awareness of the product also increases.

Through trunk shows and the physical presence of the top management in retail stores for a few days during the week, the company developed effectively in the American market. Today it represents about 40% of the company's turnover. In addition, through the experience gained in the US context, the company has expanded its international sales. This development method has been repeated for other foreign markets and has also allowed growth in Europe, representing about 20% of the market and the Russian market, which also accounts for 20% of the market. However, it is necessary to highlight how the international approach requires a considerable commercial effort to follow customers and guarantee customization. These activities are currently managed directly by the owner's top management. Therefore, the ability to listen to the end customer is one of the fundamental skills of the brand and the family that underlies it.

In addition, the development in foreign markets has beneficiated by word of mouth. Given the unique characteristics of the product and the long-lasting nature of relations with foreign customers, the company has obtained appreciation that has allowed it to expand the portfolio of end consumers served. Thus, it is a gradual growth mechanism that, over time, has expanded the range of international markets in which the brand is present.

The brand has also invested in the digital channel, with the website and presence in social networks. To date, it has developed its property website in English. The site is primarily informative since it allows to know the history, characteristics of the company's products and productions. It also refers to the presence of the products in the various retail outlets in foreign markets that allow their purchase. The digital channel, also by the company's size, is still growing, although it is part of a business model that still requires personal contact with the customer.

5.4.4 The Personal Relationships with Foreign Clients Fueling the Business Model

The set of relationships established with customers is a fundamental dimension of the business model that deserves specific reflection. Nevertheless, the brand has managed over time to maintain stable relationships that go beyond the commercial dimension. Interaction with customers is also a personal relationship, which is considered friendship. Two ways feed the relationship. On the one hand, even with his family, the entrepreneur often travels to find opportunities to visit customers in foreign destination markets. Nevertheless, on the other hand, both final consumers and retailers decide to visit the company and its laboratory when they are in Italy to appreciate the quality of the products and observe the place of origin of the shoes. For example, in the case of participation in fairs in Italy, some customers find a way to go to Montegranaro. It represents a moment of interaction that allows the company to show the artisan nature and the exclusive quality of its products. Given this, customers become a "circle of friends" in corporate jargon, precisely because the relationship with customers is a relationship of friendship other than having a commercial nature. Although, on closer inspection, as in the case of the first and second generation, the made-to-measure shoe was destined for a circle of friends-customers mainly locally, today the company, with the third generation, retraces the same approach, but having a club of friends which also includes customer-friends in international markets.

In conclusion, the Bontoni case is the case of a small company Made in Italy that has been able to find its place in the international luxury market. The commercial skills combined with the manufacturing skills held by the brand allow a match between customer needs and the potential of the company offers. The value proposition is based on Montegranaro's artisan traditions and on a family that is their custodian. These aspects strongly characterize the business model. In this scenario, the brand's ability to maintain personal relationships with its customers helps fuel growth, allowing both to appreciate production excellence and to feed the market's knowledge background. Therefore, the business model mixes traditional elements and innovative aspects in the proposal, which find

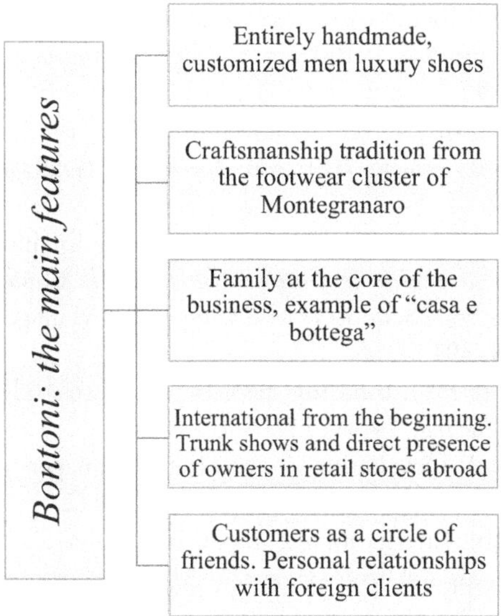

Fig. 5.2 Bontoni in pills: the main features emerging from the case. (Source: Authors' elaboration)

an element of synthesis in customization. Finally, listening to the customer is considered a fundamental asset that the company holds, allowing it to operate effectively and guide its future path. The main features emerging from the case of Bontoni are shown in Fig. 5.2.

References

Aage, T., & Belussi, F. (2008). From fashion to design: Creative networks in industrial districts. *Industry and Innovation, 15*(5), 475–491.

Barratt, M., Choi, T. Y., & Li, M. (2011). Qualitative case studies in operations management: Trends, research outcomes, and future research implications. *Journal of Operations Management, 29*(4), 329–342.

Berger, S. (2005). *How we compete: What companies around the world are doing to make it in today's global economy*. Doubleday.

Carmignani, G. (2016). Lean supply chain model and application in an Italian fashion luxury company. In *Understanding the lean enterprise* (pp. 203–220). Springer.

Cutrini, E. (2011). Moving eastwards while remaining embedded: The case of the Marche footwear district, Italy. *European Planning Studies, 19*(6), 991–1019.

Dei Ottati, G. (2004). The remarkable resilience of the industrial districts of Tuscany. *Regional Innovation Systems: The Role of Governance in a Globalized World, 2*, 21–42.

Easton, G. (1995). Case research as a methodology for industrial networks: a realist apologia. *Proceedings from the 11th IMP Conference*, Manchester, Manchester Federal School of Business and Management, Manchester (1995), pp. 368–391.

Eisenhardt, K. M. (1989). Building theories from case study research. *Academy of Management Review, 14*(4), 532–550.

Guercini, S. (2004a). Developing the researcher-manager interface in the case analysis process. *Management Decision, 42*, 464–472.

Guercini, S. (2004b). International competitive change and strategic behaviour of Italian textile-apparel firms. *Journal of Fashion Marketing and Management, 8*, 320–339.

Guercini, S., & Woodside, A. G. (2012). A strategic supply chain approach: consortium marketing in the Italian leatherwear industry. *Marketing Intelligence & Planning, 30*(7), 700–716.

Jones, R. M. (2002). *The apparel industry*. Blackwell.

Lazzeretti, L., & Capone, F. (2016). How proximity matters in innovation networks dynamics along the cluster evolution. A study of the high technology applied to cultural goods. *Journal of Business Research, 69*(12), 5855–5865.

Merlo, E. (2018). Italian luxury goods industry on the move: SMEs and global value chains. In *Global luxury* (pp. 39–63). Palgrave.

Milanesi, M., Guercini, S., & Tunisini, A. (2020). Exploring SMEs' qualitative growth and networking through formalization. *Competitiveness Review, 30*(4), 397–415.

Miles, M. B., & Huberman, A. M. (1994). *Qualitative data analysis. An expanded sourcebook*. Sage.

Paris, I. (2010). Fashion as a system: Changes in demand as the basis for the establishment of the Italian fashion system (1960–1970). *Enterprise & Society, 11*, 524–559.

Sammarra, A., & Belussi, F. (2006). Evolution and relocation in fashion-led Italian districts: Evidence from two case-studies. *Entrepreneurship and Regional Development, 18*(6), 543–562.

Settembrini, L. (1994). From haute couture to pret-a-porter. In *The Italian metamorphosis* (p. 485).

Yin, R. K. (1989). *Case study research: Design and methods* (Rev. ed.). Sage.

6

The Internationalization of Luxury Fashion SMEs After a Path of Dimensional Growth

6.1 Premise to Cases

This chapter presents four cases of medium-sized companies. Two of them belong to the luxury womenswear sector. The Italian women's clothing industry (including outerwear, knitwear, shirts, and leather clothing) remains characterized by a positive trend, mainly attributable to the performance achieved across borders. Based on the data released by Sistema Moda Italia (2020a) and elaborated by Confindustria Moda, the turnover of the sector recorded an increase of +4.5%; compared to the previous year, womenswear earned almost 600 million euros, approaching 14 billion euros. Within the Italian textile-fashion chain, womenswear plays a leading role, ensuring 24.9% of the total turnover generated. In 2019, the positive trend affected all the sectors of women's fashion, albeit with different tones; in particular, tailoring (which, it should be remembered, accounts for 59.5% of women's fashion) records a growth of +2.1%, knitwear reaches a rate of +9.9%, shirts marks a variation of +3.3%, and finally, the skincare slows down to +0.5%. Regarding the value of production carried out in Italy (variable calculated net of income deriving from the marketing of imported products), the sector balance

A. Runfola et al., *Internationalization of Luxury Fashion Firms*, Palgrave Advances in Luxury, https://doi.org/10.1007/978-3-030-88755-1_6

showed a recovery compared to the decrease in 2018, up to +0.3% on an annual basis.

Confirming the most recent market trends, domestic demand for Italian women's fashion remained reflective, while foreign demand once again proved to be particularly favorable, as has been continuous since 2010. Specifically, in 2019, sales on the international markets grew, with an annual increase of +6.1%, and reached 8979 million euros, thus contributing to 64.4% of the sectoral turnover. Regarding 2020, the data available today on the first six months are inevitably conditioned by the outbreak of the COVID-19 pandemic, which strongly affected the fashion industry (Runfola et al., 2021) in Italy and in the rest of the world, due to the interconnectedness of the global fashion market and fashion supply chains (Chakraborty & Biswas, 2020). From S/S 2019 to F/W 2019–20, the women's fashion sell-out in Italy dropped -3.1%. From January to June 2020, women's fashion exports fell -23.6%, in line with the textile-clothing supply chain as a whole (-24.2%). Compared to the first half of 2019, exports burned over 1 billion euros. Focusing the analysis on exports, after a first two months that started favorably (+1.8%), the COVID-19 pandemic certainly did not spare womenswear. The month of March 2020 dropped -4.9% compared to March 2019, and April turned out to be much worse, losing -73.3% on a trend basis. Analyzing the performance by geographical macro-area, in the case of exports, the intra-EU area on average recorded a less negative trend (-19.5%) than non-EU areas (-26.6%); in the case of imports, the intra-EU decreased, equal to -24.1%, exceeded the non-EU one of -18.7%.

The other two cases in the chapter concern luxury childrenswear and sartorial ties (Sistema Moda Italia, 2020b). The four cases are representative of medium-sized Italian luxury companies that, over the years, have achieved excellent results in terms of dimensional growth and international expansion, with a constant orientation toward relevant issues such as digitalization and sustainability, and through significant investments in distribution channels, albeit with specific traits and positioning in different segments (womenswear, menswear, childrenswear).

6.2 Fabiana Filippi: A Story of an Authentic Made in Italy and Sustainable Luxury Fashion Brand[1]

6.2.1 The Origin of the Brand and Its Philosophy

Fabiana Filippi is a fashion brand that bases its success on the story of a family, a remarkable Made in Italy product, and an international essence. The company is also characterized by a sustainable approach to the luxury market, with a broad vision of sustainability that includes all economic, social, and ecological dimensions and that involves all business processes and the relationship with the various stakeholders. This attention to the values of sustainability has distinguished it from birth. Fabiana Filippi is a women's clothing and accessories brand in the luxury segment, with a particular vocation for cashmere knitwear. The company creates, produces, and distributes its collections through a philosophy that manages the entire production chain and creates clothing and accessories characterized by a high-end positioning in the contemporary luxury segment. The Fabiana Filippi collection combines sophisticated, high-quality materials, Italian know-how, and contemporary design. The brand represents a case of excellence of Made in Italy, and over the years, it has managed to establish itself internationally for the values it bears and, of course, for the style and quality of its productions. The concept of Made in Italy relies on the traditions of the local area where the company produces its products. As already stated, the brand relies on a sustainable approach to the luxury market. So then, sustainability, along with quality, is a pillar of the company brand.

The growth path of the brand has been constant for over thirty years of life. It reached 90 million euros turnover in 2019, while it was roughly 20 million euros in 2009. The company philosophy fueled this growth. Fabiana Filippi demonstrates how a company with strong and authentic

[1] The case is written by Andrea Runfola. The case is based on secondary data and information gathered by means of several interviews and meetings with the Founder and President of the company Mario Filippi Coccetta. A company visit was also done by the author. We thank Mario Filippi Coccetta for kind availability and for sharing information about the company.

values can represent a benchmark for other fashion and luxury industry players. Thanks to the results reached, in terms of business performance and the contribution to sustainable development, the founder and CEO of the company, Mario Filippi Coccetta, in 2018, received by the President of the Italian Republic the Order of Merit for Labour, becoming a *Cavaliere del Lavoro*. The President of the Italian Republic assigns the Order of Merit for Labour to entrepreneurs who have distinguished themselves in Italy and is an extraordinary honor for business people.

The company proposes itself as a significant player in the international panorama of women's luxury and distributes its collections in over forty foreign markets. It is an example of how a company becomes a recognized luxury player with an international awareness starting from a small-medium size.

The company has its origins in the Umbria region's heart, particularly in the small village of Giano dell'Umbria. The company's location is within a rural geographical area with a strong heritage in knitwear processing and the sartorial traditions of the handmade. The company interprets this heritage and proposes itself as an actor capable of enhancing and supporting the skills acquired and established in the territory. The company is the guarantor of the sartorial and craft traditions of the area, both by collaborating with local suppliers (represented by small workshops) and by training young staff in knitwear and tailoring. Protecting local knowledge is a distinctive feature of the company and its proposal and represents at the same time a sustainability dimension of its business model.

The story of Fabiana Filippi is that of a family, which comes from farmer origins and decides to create a fashion brand that finds its roots in the tradition of Umbrian cashmere knitwear. It takes inspiration also from the natural beauty, cultural and architectural aspects of the region and that of Italy as a whole.

The company's origin dates back to 1985 when two brothers, Mario and Giacomo Filippi Coccetta, together with Donatella, Giacomo's wife, decided to create a workshop in the agricultural shed where their father worked. It represented an ambitious project whose idea was to interpret the know-how of handmade and craftsmanship in a modern key, which in Umbria was represented by the strong culture of knitwear. The tradition of knitwear in Umbria was born between the First and Second World Wars. Therefore, the idea of the two brothers was to start from this culture and reinterpret it in a modern key, making it become an international business. This vocation for export has been one of the brand's distinctive features right from the start, given that foreign markets have immediately absorbed over 70% of production.

The company connects the brand to the traditions of the land and the peasant tradition from its origins. This fundamental element of the company's DNA remains today, considering that Fabiana Filippi, now a significant player in the luxury fashion scene, maintains its main headquarters in a rural area. The Umbria Region also has one of its strengths in the rural tradition since it is also famous for its food production, such as olive oil and wine. The linkages with the territory are essential for the brand. The connection also fuels the sustainable approach to the fashion industry developed over the years.

In addition, as anticipated, one of the aspects of the link with the territory concerns the influence of the architectural, cultural, landscape, and natural beauties of the Umbria region, and in general, of Italy. The fact of remaining anchored and working in places marked by peculiar characteristics makes beauty a source of inspiration, which contaminates and influences the work and, therefore, the product conceived by the brand. Furthermore, the company supports cultural initiatives in the area, such as, among others, the sponsorship of an important international festival, "Festival dei Due Mondi" in a nearby city within the region, Spoleto. Similarly, in 2021, the company decided to donate part of the revenues from organic cotton collections to support the non-profit organization FAI (Fondo Ambiente Italiano) in maintaining the Saint Francis forest in Assisi. This Umbrian city is a world-leading religious and tourism destination.

Furthermore, in 2021, it launched the project "Terra" to achieve sustainable development goals. These initiatives aim to give back to the territory and maintain the beauties, both landscape and culture, with which the company interacts. Similarly, the company launched the project "Light Up the Future" which includes social sustainability initiatives. Additionally, in 2020 to contribute to the fight against the pandemic,

Fabiana Filippi donated machinery to the local hospitals of Foligno and Spoleto and face masks to operators of some institutions.

Therefore, these dimensions of connection with the territory also permeate the approach to sustainability, given that Fabiana Filippi can be considered an authentic Made in Italy company by a firmly anchored and localized production process and sustainable from birth. Furthermore, the product offered is the result of a "cosy minimalism" (source: company website) in which much attention is paid to raw materials and processing skills from a sustainable perspective, with "respect for the earth and people", states the CEO. A series of values characterize the company, which describes them, as part of its mission, with keywords such as trust, respect, ethics, excellence, gift, honesty, and improvement (the initials of the words in Italian give rise to the word "freedom", an acronym that summarizes them).

After its foundation in 1985, the company led by the two brothers (Mario and Giacomo) and the wife of Giacomo (Donatella Filippi), initially operated as sub-supplier; in the meantime, a process of structuring begins with the inclusion of personnel assigned to critical activities such as design, modeling, the technical-production dimension, which will lead it in a few years to propose its collection of clothing. It was in 1990 that the company launched the first collection with the Fabiana Filippi brand. Fabiana is the name of the daughter of Giacomo and Donatella. Since then, a growth path has begun that will lead it to be, as already anticipated, an emblematic case of Made in Italy luxury success at an international level.

6.2.2 The Product, the Target, and the Production Process

Fabiana Filippi brand, as anticipated, was launched in 1990 as a cashmere knitwear brand. In 2004, however, it decided to expand its offer, proposing a total look for a female target. Mario Filippi Coccetta defines the Fabiana Filippi product as "beautiful and well made", with a critical role, as already mentioned, played by craftsmanship. As pointed out, the "beautiful and well made" product can have an international value and therefore find appreciation in the luxury segment. The brand describes its collections as composed of garments inspired by "simplicity", intended as the maximum expression of refinement. Simplicity is a term that recalls the themes of concreteness, precision, and refinement. The company offers garments that make consumers feel at ease and allow the target to express their personality on various occasions of the day. The Fabiana Filippi product is a product designed and created to last over time. Timeless beauty is a concept that guides the culture of being the head of the brand. "What is beautiful today remains beautiful over time", explains Mario Filippi Coccetta. This concept incorporates simplicity recalled previously.

In addition, the company has always paid particular attention to sustainability as an element that characterizes its business model, and this aspect characterizes all stages of the creation and production process and the distribution of clothing.

Over time, the company has heavily invested in innovation, creativity, research into materials, the enhancement of craftsmanship, and how to combine craftsmanship with new technologies.

Design, research, and creative ability are critical skills of the company. An internal style office manages the design of the collections. The target woman of Fabiana Filippi shows a series of characteristics such as elegance, personality, commitment, and internationality. The brand has always proposed an "international" vocation, to which it links the manufacturing traditions of the region. In particular, the Fabiana Filippi consumer pays particular attention to detail, the types of craft and expresses her being in a luxury product that is not ostentatious. This aspect is a central dimension of the brand. It aims to create products that allow its target to combine the aesthetics and design of a luxury product with elements that allow its functionality, even in the life of all days. On closer inspection, the minimalist dimension of the brand in these terms reflects the desire to represent a quality product aimed at a target interested in learning about the company's history and making its values their own. As is well highlighted, however, the target consumer does not choose the brand because she wants to be represented by a logo but instead chooses the brand because it helps her feel better and express herself on every occasion of use during the day.

The selection of raw materials is the object of particular attention. They are mainly natural fibers, including in addition to cashmere, silk, linen, and cotton. It is significant that concerning this aspect, the company also undertakes to maintain for part of the production garments with natural colors of the raw materials to avoid dyeing. As already specified, the approach to sustainability also concerns aspects related to the product, such as labels, hangers, and packaging made with biodegradable products.

The company manages all the production process steps from conception, design, and manufacturing of each item and the logistics dimension. Part of the production is carried out internally at the Giano dell'Umbria headquarter, but the company also entrusts the production to external laboratories, about 300. The external laboratories are almost entirely located in Umbria and are small in size, while the remaining part of the laboratories is, in any case, located in Italy. Then, the company activates collaborations aimed at maintaining the local productive fabric. The sustainability of the production process also regards the company's ability to reduce the waste of raw materials. For example, the company implemented the "fully fashioned" system since the brand's launch, using machinery that allows avoiding waste in knitwear production, which is the assortment's core business. Similarly, it implements the "optimized placement of patterns" in the tailoring activities. Since the launch of the brand, these aspects have characterized the company's production and allowed the company to be one of the pioneers in reducing the environmental impact of its activities.

It is also interesting to note the company's continuous investment in technologies to support the craftsmanship dimension. For example, in 2020, Fabiana Filippi inaugurated a fully mechanized logistics center of over 4000 square meters in Giano dell'Umbria. It was an Industry 4.0 investment. It represented an opportunity to integrate the latest technologies within the current technological paradigms of the industrial revolution, combining them within a process that keeps local know-how at the center.

6.2.3 The International Dimension of the Business Model

Internationalization is a component of the corporate business model. As previously highlighted, the Fabiana Filippi brand has been an international brand since its inception, given that foreign markets have represented the majority of turnover since the launch in the 1990s. The company now operates in various international markets and is present in over forty countries, including European markets, the American market, and the APAC (Asia Pacific) countries. Italy accounts for about 23%, Europe about 26%, while for over 50% the company allocates its collections to markets outside the EU.

The approach to foreign markets has evolved following the company's growth path and the evolution of the luxury fashion business. Therefore, the company has managed to integrate the internationalization dimension into its business model, adapting its internationality to the market's needs.

At the time of the brand's launch, in 1990, the first international market targeted was Japan. Then, thanks to the participation of the top owner in an international fair, he reached sales agreements with customers of the wholesale channel. From that moment, a path began, which also considered the typical development methods of the fashion of those years, such as the importance of trade fairs, saw the company participate in international events in various locations to reach wholesale customers in various locations of the high-end segment. At the same time, the development abroad in those years makes use of the collaboration with agents, which allowed reaching intermediate customers in foreign markets. The international wholesale clientele therefore grows, and so does the visibility of the brand on foreign markets.

Of course, as stated by the CEO, these ways of approaching international markets change with the company's growth and with the reputation acquired by the brand. As a result, the company begins to manage the phases of connection with wholesale customers directly. For example, it opened its executive showrooms to welcome distributors, present collections, and collect orders. At the same time, the brand develops its own sales organization both in the corporate headquarters and in the various operating offices that, over time, are created in some foreign markets.

The change in the approach to foreign markets also provides a more significant company presence in distribution activities. As a result, the brand implemented new distribution channels according to an omnichannel logic.

To date, the distribution of products both nationally and internationally takes place through three channels: wholesale channel, retail channel, and e-commerce (both proprietary and through third-party e-commerce platforms).

The wholesale channel has historically represented and still represents the primary mode of distribution. The company turns to highly prestigious multi-brand retail customers for the distribution of its collections. As is well known, this is an indirect distribution method, which the company oversees through its sales force and which in 2019 represented almost 80% of turnover. The wholesale channel is essential for overseeing international markets and expanding opportunities in terms of potential target segments. In addition, the use of the wholesale channel allows a comparison with major players in fashion, a comparison that also allows the company to verify and adapt the strategies implemented. To date, there are about 1100 wholesale customers, a number that demonstrates the brand's ability to find an appreciation of its collections by distributors.

Alongside the wholesale channel, in 2010, the company launched the retail project. Considering the awareness achieved in the international luxury market, it decides to develop its distribution network, which has provided for opening single-brand stores both in Italy and abroad. The first store opened in 2010 is in Forte dei Marmi, a famous resort town in Italy, followed in 2012 by the stores in Milan and London. Over the years, the company has made increasing investments in its retail strategy. As a result, the company now has over eighty single-brand stores in a plurality of international markets. The management of the stores (partly directly managed and partly in franchising) takes place both directly from the headquarters in Giano dell'Umbria and through its subsidiaries in foreign markets. In fact, in some foreign markets, the company has operating units that it controls and deals with the management of retail outlets. The retail channel generates around 18% of turnover (in 2019) and has seen extraordinary growth over the last few years. In addition, it represented a way to strengthen the brand image, allowing a direct relationship with the final consumer. In this way, the consumer can get to know the world of Fabiana Filippi, coming into direct contact with the brand.

Furthermore, in 2016, the company decided to launch its e-commerce site dedicated to online sales. The online channel integrates with the presence in international markets, given that the markets where the company has a higher presence are also those that generate more sales on the e-commerce site. The investment in the e-commerce channel also provided for a strengthening of the digital communication activities to support the site, especially during 2020 in response to the pandemic period. In addition, alongside the proprietary e-commerce site, the company also recurs to online multi-brand retailers (e-commerce platforms), which allow it to expand the target base in terms of customers. Combining online and third-party presence can let the company reach a broad audience. As in the case of wholesale customers, also, in this case, the company is targeting prestigious players in the online luxury market.

Ultimately, the distribution strategy of the products comprises a plurality of distribution channels both nationally and internationally. The same goes for communication channels, which integrate traditional offline media, such as advertising campaigns on major international newspapers and new digital channels.

As highlighted, the approach to international markets now provides almost direct supervision of the company through the channels described. Also, in consideration of this, in 2018, the company inaugurated a second headquarter in Milan. The new headquarter covering roughly 2400 square meters aims to represent a bridge between Umbria and the rest of the world, as stated by Mario Filippi Coccetta. It includes a showroom and hosts some units of the company. However, the headquarter in Umbria remains the main seat of the company's activities.

In conclusion, the Fabiana Filippi brand represents an emblematic case of a company's ability to develop in the luxury fashion market internationally. It is an entrepreneurial story from a family that carries out its work with passion, transmits this passion to all stakeholders, and naturally transfers it to the market. Furthermore, it is a story that includes people, collaborators, and employees who have shared the business experience. In this scenario, the brand has carved out space in contemporary luxury with a particular product philosophy regarding the offer and target. Moreover, its natural vocation to sustainability issues represents another strength of the company within the luxury landscape. The main features of the case are shown in Fig. 6.1.

Fig. 6.1 Fabiana Filippi in pills: the main features emerging from the case. (Source: Authors' elaboration)

6.3 Antonelli Firenze: Family, Territory, and Design in the Luxury Womenswear[2]

6.3.1 The Origin of the Brand and the Business Model

Antonelli Firenze is a brand held by a historic company, Gossip, located in Castelfiorentino, in the province of Florence, and founded in 1950, initially under the name Vicad, by Luciano Antonelli. In the beginning, the company produced household linen and nightdresses, then moving on to jersey shirts. An important step in the company's history took place in 2001 with the generational handover to the daughters Enrica and Roberta. The company inaugurated a new chapter in its history and launched the first collection of women's couture shirts with the brand Gossip, immediately obtaining wide acclaim not only in the domestic market but also abroad, where the company began to sell through a network of agents in multi-brand stores, especially in Northern Europe. The two sisters explain that having gained experience in the field with the production of shirts has allowed them to acquire a culture of fine fabrics and their numerous variations, but also to develop creativity through the search for unusual combinations of fabrics and processes.

As early as 2008, the brand recorded a further evolution, defining its positioning in the accessible luxury segment, with products distributed in over 500 multi-brand stores in Italy and abroad. In the same year, the third entrepreneurial generation arrived in the company with Marco Berni, Enrica's son, with a position of Marketing and Financial Director first, and then CEO. Over the years, the will to expand the collection to a total look has increased. The real turning point came in 2013 when the brand Gossip was replaced by Antonelli Firenze. The choice of the name is not accidental: on the one hand, it highlights the family origins of the brand; on the other hand, it underlines the clear territorial origin as well as the Made in Italy essence.

---

[2] The case is written by Matilde Milanesi. The case is based on secondary data and information gathered by means of interviews with the CEO of the company Marco Berni. A company visit was also done by the author. We thank Marco Berni for kind availability and for sharing information about the company.

Antonelli Firenze, therefore, offers a total look defined as "by women for women", whose stylistic vision is innovative and constantly looking for natural elegance, without excesses, and with an Italian imprint. The typical target of the brand is a working and independent woman, who buys clothes with clean lines and sober elegance in search of a luxury given by design, raw materials, and workmanship, but never ostentatious. The brand is aimed at a transversal target in terms of age, based on the assumption that quality collections, entirely produced in Italy, can intercept even the needs of younger women.

Visiting the historic factory in the heart of the town of Castelfiorentino, one recognizes the strong territorial roots and the typical trait of a family business, both elements recognized as the strength of the brand. In the plant, there are the management center, the stylistic phases, raw materials, and finished products, the development of the samples. Recently, the cutting phase was also entirely internalized and supported by the purchase of two new machines. The raw materials are entirely purchased in Italy, in particular in the historic textile district of the Tuscan city of Prato, where there is a deep-rooted tradition of producing top-quality fabrics aimed at Italian and international fashion and luxury brands.

The production of the collections is Made in Italy, mainly made in the same region, Tuscany, since the company uses a dense network of qualified local suppliers, with few exceptions, such as a supplier located in India for some specific processes. The family business structure, characterized by fluidity and speed in decision-making and anticipating trends and changes, combined with a consolidated network of local suppliers capable of guaranteeing rapid delivery and high standards in processing, represent key factors of the business model. These key features allow the company to be innovative, adopt a proactive approach, and, concerning the distribution, guarantee a streamlined restocking service in just twenty-four hours in all countries.

6.3.2 The Company Growth and Recent Evolution

The results of the company's strategic choices were not long in coming, with constant increases in turnover and EBIT in recent years. The year

2017, for example, was a particularly positive year, with a jump in turnover of 30% more than the previous year. More generally, the positive performances achieved in recent years are also due to an optimization process linked to a reduction in inefficiencies in the production structure, and the sale of products with higher stylistic value. Surprisingly, even 2020, the year of the global COVID-19 pandemic, marked an important growth for the company, which went from a turnover of around €12.8 million in 2019 to around €15.5 million in 2020, with profit growth. The growth is attributable to various factors, such as the growing attention to collections and design, which is increasingly refined and distinguishable. This led to an excellent result in terms of sell-out in the multi-brand stores where the brand is sold, exceeding 85% even before the start of the sales. At the same time, the weight of foreign markets and their penetration has grown, also through online channels.

It should be noted that during the pandemic emergency resulting from the spread of the COVID-19 virus, the company was able to quickly reconvert its business by producing surgical masks and obtaining the necessary certifications for sale. This activity, after the end of the first wave of the virus in Italy in May 2020, continued with excellent results and was added to the main production of women's clothing. Therefore, the negative effects of the pandemic on the fashion sector, due to the suspension of sales in the months when all activities were closed, were offset with this initiative. The production of masks involved a production system to be revolutionized and, above all, a long phase of the study and testing for the production and marketing of type 2 surgical masks, which can be used in the hospitals and COVID-19 divisions. The company was the first in Tuscany (seventh in Italy out of over 800 companies) to obtain the green light from the Istituto Superiore di Sanità,[3] starting production as early as March.

As the CEO points out, the company had to face the legal stop to fashion production during the first lockdown in Italy. The goal was to immediately look for a possible system to safeguard the economic

[3] The Istituto Superiore di Sanità (Italian National Institute of Health), also ISS, is an Italian public institution that is the leading technical-scientific body of the Italian National Health Service and performs research, trials, control, counseling, documentation and training for public health.

sustainability of the company and support the thirty-five employees. The production of masks since the beginning of the pandemic represents a clear example of the "fluidity and dynamism" of the company, as underlined by the CEO, as well as its rapid decision-making ability aimed at recognizing opportunities even in times of difficulty.

Finally, two other elements characterize the company. The first is growing attention to the digital world, which has been approached with caution but will represent one of the main investments for the next few years, accompanied by in-company training and the recruitment of specialized managers. To date, Antonelli Firenze focuses on its website, in which it has been recently added a digital store to sell a wide selection of the current season. The goal was, therefore, to open a sales channel complementary to traditional retail, to offer a purchase opportunity to all markets, especially the European ones in which the company is already present. At the same time, the role of social networks is primary, in particular Instagram, in which there is a goal of growth in the coming years, also through influencer marketing campaigns that blend well with the brand identity. However, it is highlighted that the presence in digital channels must necessarily go hand in hand with attention to the product, its design, materials, and processing techniques, elements considered fundamental for the brand, in priority compared to online and offline communication.

A second key element is attention to some issues related to sustainability, in particular the economic-financial one, particularly relevant for the CEO who brought his financial background and his profound knowledge of financial statements to the company. Social sustainability is also in the spotlight, aimed at maintaining and job creation in the Florentine territory, both through direct employees and in local supply chains. Sustainability is also related to ethics and attention to animal welfare since the company was among the first in Italy to eliminate the use of furs from production.

6.3.3 The International Expansion

Over the years, internationalization has represented a natural growth path for Antonelli Firenze. Women's luxury clothing, such as that proposed by the company, finds a fundamental outlet in foreign markets because domestic demand would not be able to support the survival and development of the company. In addition, the company has always had a vocation toward exports and is aimed at a type of woman with strong international traits. The change of the brand, from Gossip to Antonelli Firenze, also took place with a view to better accommodating the tastes of an international clientele and positioning the brand more strongly in the luxury segment. Foreign markets currently account for around 70% of turnover.

The main foreign markets are Germany, Switzerland, Belgium, Austria, markets in which the company can have a higher markup on products. The taste of the consumers of those countries in terms of fashion fits perfectly with the style, design, and non-ostentatious luxury that the brand offers. In Germany, for example, in just three seasons after the change of brand, Antonelli Firenze has come to serve sixty customers (multi-brand stores). Japan, the United States, the United Kingdom, South Korea, and recently Russia are also experiencing interesting growth.

The company sells its products in a large network of luxury multi-brand stores, many of which are long-standing and strong loyal customers. In the United States, for example, Antonelli Firenze sells in over fifty luxury multi-brand stores throughout the territory, which are considered a fundamental step in consolidating its presence in the area before boosting growth on the market and entering large chains such as Neiman Marcus.

Commercial penetration abroad is supported by a network of multi-mandate agents, a fundamental resource for the company for the promotion of commercial contracts between the company and foreign customers, and also for the in-depth knowledge of foreign markets held by the agents. Foreign markets have been the real engine of the brand's growth. An example was the year 2015, when Antonelli Firenze recorded a growth of 18% compared to the previous year, with an EBITDA of 12.7%, mainly due to the increase in the export share in Germany, Switzerland,

Belgium, countries of the Scandinavian Peninsula and France. The following year, foreign markets further grew by about 70%, with a gradual improvement in margins.

Emerging markets are also an important destination for the brand. Recently, Russia has become an interesting market for the growth of the company, which has opened a pop-up store in Moscow. On the one hand, this represents an important entry into a historically relevant country for all Italian fashion and luxury brands; on the other hand, it represents a first step toward the opening of single-brand stores abroad. The store in Russia was opened with the support of a local partner, given the geographical and cultural distance of the Russian market. The opening of single-brand stores is a relevant issue, albeit not a priority for the company. The network of agents currently allows excellent penetration into foreign markets with lower investments than those that would entail the opening of single-brand stores, especially if managed directly.

The company is continuing its expansion into emerging markets. A relevant example is a five-year agreement with the Korean group Parco International for the opening of seven single-brand shop-in-shops in major Korean department stores, with the prospect of reaching ten based on turnover. South Korea was selected as particularly inclined to appreciate Made in Italy, and as the gateway to the brand in the Far East area, where Japan is also a relevant market for the opening of single-brand stores with a local partner. An agreement was signed with the L'Idea & Co group, a Japanese group that controls the Strasbourg chain of stores, for the opening of a series of shop-in-shops, three of which are in Tokyo. In addition, internationalization also goes through the online channel. Antonelli Firenze website is currently translated into English and German, and the e-commerce section in Italian and English has just been inaugurated. At the same time, the company sells its products in online multi-brand retailers, which today represent an important showcase for many Made in Italy luxury brands. Two notable examples are represented by Yoox and Fartfetch.

In conclusion, Antonelli Firenze is a Made in Italy brand with a strong identity and positioning in luxury fashion, whose fundamental features can be summarized in the following points (see also Fig. 6.2):

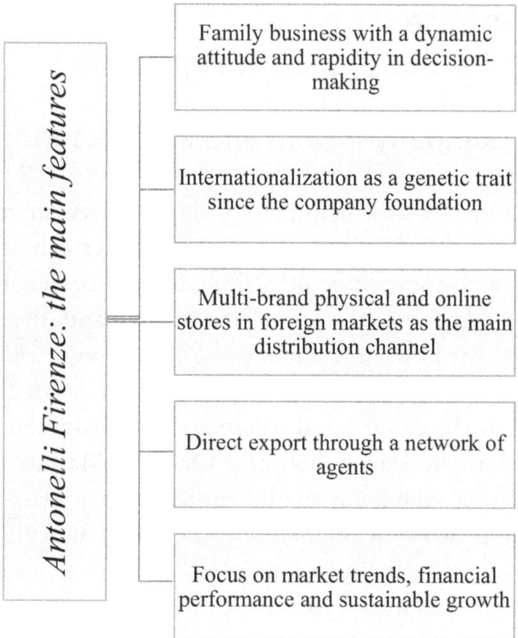

Fig. 6.2 Antonelli Firenze in pills: the main features emerging from the case. (Source: Authors' elaboration)

- Family business characterized by dynamism, fluidity, rapid decision-making, traits that make the company capable of anticipating changes and seizing opportunities even in difficulties.
- Link with the territory of origin of the company, where the headquarters and the supply chain are located.
- Constant attention to product design, which represents the main strength of the offer.
- "Genetic" internationalization since the company's origins, through direct export made possible by a consolidated network of agents who promote sales in multi-brand stores.
- Monitoring of market trends, such as digitalization and e-commerce, while always keeping an eye on the financial performance of the company and its sustainable growth.

6.4 Monnalisa and the Luxury Childrenswear[4]

6.4.1 The Company Profile and Business Model

The junior fashion (which includes clothing, underwear, and accessories for the age group 0–14) represents a relevant sector for Made in Italy fashion, albeit with some difficulties linked to sector dynamics. This segment is populated by several actors. On the one hand, there are the adult fashion brands that have now entered the junior segment en masse and, driven by the distributive firepower of the big brands, are increasing sales and exports. On the other hand, there are big chains such as Zara and H&M, as well as the Italian Ovs and Original Marines, which attract consumers with affordable prices and contemporary style.

Between these two blocks, there are the companies that have always specialized in junior fashion, which, in Italy, are fewer and fewer and see the traditional distribution channels (independent multi-brand stores) shrink every year, suffer from the (persistent) decline in consumption on the market internally, and try to make their way abroad, the only driving force of the sector. Despite a difficult scenario, the data released by Sistema Moda Italia (2020b) and elaborated by Confindustria Moda on the occasion of Pitti Bimbo, the main childrenswear trade fair in Europe, indicate a turnover in 2019 up +3.5% which, for the first time, exceeded 3 billion thanks to the driving force of exports: +6.1% foreign sales, whose weight rose from 40.1 to 41.2%. However, in 2019 imports grew faster, leading to a worsening of the trade balance and a negative result of 850 million. In the same year, on the distribution front, in Italy, the independent store channel lost another 4.4%, to the advantage of outlets (+155%) and street vendors (+17%), while online sales decreased (-7.9%).

Even a historic company, such as Monnalisa, the only listed junior fashion company (on the Aim market of the Italian stock exchange),

[4] The case is written by Matilde Milanesi. The case is based on secondary data gathered by the authors, including company website, investor relations report and news appeared in fashion magazines.

which has always focused on its brand and exports, has highlighted, through the words of its CEO Christian Simoni, that the current situation is the worst one for junior clothing in the last twenty years, with wholesale distribution in a serious crisis in many areas of the world, such as Hong Kong, Russia, and the United Arab Emirates. Fortunately, Monnalisa, in the last four years, has turned to retail, investing more than 30 million euros in the direct distribution channel, and is now waiting for the positive performance of the stores in the start-up phase, closing 2019 with a turnover in line with the previous year (47.9 million euros).

Despite the great difficulties of the year 2020, which, due to the COVID-19 pandemic, recorded a loss of turnover in the junior fashion sector of over 13%, Monnalisa faced 2020 with determination, contributing with an important donation to support the COVID-19 emergency in the city of Arezzo (Tuscany), and by producing TNT masks. The pandemic emergency was not lenient even with the historic company, which closed 2020 with revenues down by 30% compared to the previous year. The distribution of revenues by this channel recorded a 21% growth in the e-commerce, thanks to a precise corporate strategy that channeled the main investments by introducing important technological developments to support the digital store. The wholesale channel, considering the persistence of the pandemic crisis, recorded a decrease of 28%, while the retail channel reported a decrease of 38%.

Monnalisa was founded in Arezzo in 1968 by Piero Iacomoni, current President of the Board. The company designs, produces, and distributes luxury childrenswear (0–16 years), under the brand of the same name, through multiple distribution channels. The company philosophy has always combined entrepreneurial activity, innovation, the search for new markets, original styling, and particular attention to the development of corporate resources and skills. If innovation represents the competitive lever par excellence, to be preserved and enhanced as one of the key components of the company's intangible assets, creativity is the fulcrum of the production process. To direct the team of thirty people, the Creative Director Barbara Bertocci and her daughter Diletta Iacomoni, Fashion Coordinator. Monnalisa combines significant investments in research and development, great social sensitivity, compliance with the SA 8000 standard and ISO 14001 environmental certification, to the offer of great quality and fashion content. Since April 2016, Monnalisa has also been certified by Elite-Borsa Italiana, a program designed for the support and growth of SMEs that opened the company to new opportunities.

At a consolidated level, Monnalisa has over 300 employees and a 2019 turnover of 47.9 million euros, of which 67% was abroad, in over sixty countries. The company operates exclusively with its proprietary brand Monnalisa, with a clear positioning in luxury, strategic autonomy, and focused investments.

The company declares six fundamental pillars for its business model:

- Creativity
- Innovation
- Strong brand identity
- Investments in trend analysis and researches
- Acknowledgment of the excellence of the style team
- Designing and creating activities completely insourced

The designing and creating activities are entirely internalized and carried out through a dedicated team of thirty design and style experts. Every year, Monnalisa creates and launches two main collections (Fall-Winter and Spring-Summer) and two pre-collections. On average, each seasonal collection consists of 900 items. Furthermore, Monnalisa has an extremely flexible production structure. All the transformation phases, following the control of the raw materials and the cutting of the fabrics, are outsourced to small artisan workshops near the company where constant control activities are maintained to guarantee a high-quality level.

6.4.2 The Internationalization Process Through Physical and Online Distribution Channels

Monnalisa's growth and international development are marked by some particularly important moments in its history after the foundation in 1968. In 1975, Monnalisa participated for the first time at the International Fashion event "Pitti Bimbo", one of the most important international trade fair in the childrenswear sector. It is held annually in

Florence and represents an important showcase for brands, as the trade fair hosts buyers from all over the world. From then on, growth continued in the domestic and foreign markets. A fundamental step toward internationalization took place in 1988, the year that marked the beginning of the internationalization process with the sale of Monnalisa products in stores in Paris, New York, and London. In the year 2001, the first Corporate Responsibility Statement was released, bearing witness to the focus on issues related to corporate social responsibility and sustainability. In the 2000s, the company invested heavily in the opening of single-brand stores, such as the one in Florence that opened in 2003 and Milan that opened in 2006. In 2008, it entered the Lafayette department store in Paris, Harrods in London, and Endless Story in Moscow, continuing its international growth even further in markets as far away as Australia. Since then, the focus on opening stores has been constant, reaching forty-seven single-brand stores around the world and over 500 multi-brand stores.

In particular, Monnalisa operates globally through four distribution channels:

1. Corporate retail: direct single-brand stores, DOS, and DOO (directly operated stores/outlets).
2. Wholesale single-brand: single-brand stores in partnership TPOS (third-party operated stores) and TPSIS (third-party shop-in-shop) in top department stores.
3. Wholesale: independent multi-brand stores
4. E-commerce: single-brand and multi-brand online marketplaces

Monnalisa was one of the first companies operating in the childrenswear sector to adopt a constant growth strategy with the opening of single-brand stores, gaining a wealth of knowledge and skills in the management of distribution channels, which constitutes a solid source of competitive advantage. Characterized by a strong and growing international vocation, to increase the degree of penetration in foreign markets and the direct retail channel, since 2016 Monnalisa has established subsidiaries in the US, Russia, China, Brazil, South Korea, Taiwan, and Turkey, in addition to the operational subsidiaries of Hong Kong and three branches in Spain, France, and the UK. Currently, Monnalisa exclusively distributes its brand lines in over sixty countries (Americas, Far East/Oceania, the Middle East/Africa, Europe, Eastern Europe/Russia), both in direct flagship stores and in the most prestigious Department Stores of the world (including Harrods, la Rinascente, Galeries Lafayette, Saks Fifth Avenue, Harvey Nichols, Bloomingdales, Sogo, El Cortes Ingles, SKP, TsUM).

The retail network is constantly evolving, even during the difficult year 2020 when Monnalisa opened three shop-in-shops in Galeries Lafayette (Haussmann Paris, Nice Cap, and Nice Massena), France; two temporary stores in Japan; one new store at Marina Bay Sand in Singapore; one outlet store in Barberino (Florence, IT); one outlet store in Noventa di Piave (Venice, IT); one new store in Taiwan; one concession in Rinascente, Milan; and one TPOS in New Delhi, India. The importance of emerging markets for the international development of the company is evident.

In addition to physical distribution, e-commerce is taking on an ever-increasing role. Monnalisa was a pioneer for the e-commerce channel in the childrenswear market, being the first company in the world to open a direct e-commerce store. From a wholesale point of view, Monnalisa has signed contracts with the main e-commerce platforms, such as Childrensalon, which is a leader in the childrenswear market e-commerce, and other global luxury players, such as Luisa Via Roma, Farfetch, Mytheresa, Yoox, Melijoe, that contribute to the worldwide diffusion of the brand. Furthermore, the company is working on full integration from online to offline to implement the showrooming concept. More specifically, the fitting process takes place within the physical store, but the customer can comfortably choose to receive the product directly at home. Additionally, through the implementation of RFID (Radio-Frequency IDentification) technology, the company has made it possible to track each product to give information to the final consumer on the features of every item, the origin of the raw materials, and the production process.

More generally, digital transformation has become part of the company's DNA. Monnalisa has stepped up its digital focus, adopting a virtual showroom platform that hosted the SS21 sales campaign just after the lockdown ended, strongly promoting the collections and sharing technical, style, and inspirational details with customers—particularly those overseas who cannot travel internationally and make their seasonal showroom visit. The new virtual showrooming platform was implemented to: accelerate the time to wholesale market; facilitate the access to the showroom to clients during this COVID-19 emergency; reduce the number of collections.

The year 2020 marked a further evolution of Monnalisa's business, which entered into an agreement with Chiara Ferragni, famous Italian entrepreneur and influencer worldwide. The digital entrepreneur has signed a five-year licensing agreement with Monnalisa. The new deal aims to grow the Chiara Ferragni Collection brand worldwide, through the structure and experience of Monnalisa. Therefore, the international projection is the basis of the project. Monnalisa will take care of the conception, with the supervision and approval of the Ferragni team, the production and distribution of the children's line through its retail and e-commerce network. The Chiara Ferragni Collection will debut with the fall/winter 2021–22 season. Chiara Ferragni considers the agreement as a further step in the global development of her brand and considers Monnalisa's global excellence in luxury childrenswear, which will allow her brand to enter this market segment. The CEO of Monnalisa considers this agreement an unprecedented opportunity to decline all the creative, production, commercial, and distribution expertise, making use of important economies of scale. Monnalisa, therefore, stands as the flywheel of a young but iconic brand, benefiting at the same time from the global fame of Chiara Ferragni, also very popular with Monnalisa's young mothers, as a model of a determined woman to identify with.[5]

Internationalization represents the strategic direction for the future development of the company. In particular, in the near future of Monnalisa, there is a boost to the internationalization process through the retail and wholesale channels and the entry into new strategic markets, such as those of the Asia Pacific area, as well as further penetration of the markets already covered. The market opportunities offered by China will be exploited through a direct presence and the opening of twenty new DOS in the coming years. These openings are part of the

---

[5] https://www.pambianconews.com/2020/11/23/chiara-ferragni-affida-il-kidswear-a-monnalisa-305298/

plan that provides for another thirty new DOS in the world. In addition, Monnalisa intends to expand the travel channel through new openings in major international airports such as Istanbul, Rome, and Singapore.

To conclude, Monnalisa is a medium-sized Italian luxury childrenswear company strongly oriented toward internationalization and the opening of stores, a process that began over thirty years ago. Its business model is characterized by the orientation toward foreign markets, creativity, innovation, integration between online and offline channels, and openness to new trends in the luxury market, including digital transformation, influencer marketing, and collaborations with emerging brands. The main features of Monnalisa are shown in Fig. 6.3.

6.5 E.Marinella: An International Icon of Luxury Ties Production[6]

6.5.1 The Brand and Its Origin

E.Marinella is a historic company with a solid international reputation. It succeeded in becoming a leading player within the luxury industry during more than one century of its history. The brand is famous and appreciated in the world in particular for its proposal of luxury ties.[7] The company is one of the ambassadors of the style of Naples and is appreciated in international markets for the quality, elegance, and tailoring of its products. E.Marinella originates in a territory rich in the sartorial tradition of which it is one of the worldwide representatives. It is a family-owned company that has now reached the fourth generation of entrepreneurs. Today, father (Maurizio Marinella) and son (Alessandro

---

[6] The case is written by Andrea Runfola. The case is based on secondary data gathered by the authors, including company website and news which appeared in fashion magazines.

[7] The production of ties is part of men's fashion system. According to the estimates of the Sistema Moda Italia, Italian men's fashion in 2019 generated about 18% of the turnover of the textile-fashion industry, a percentage that increases to 28.7% if we consider only turnover from the clothing industry. Exports represent about 70% of the total turnover of the men's fashion (source: https://www.sistemamodaitalia.com/it/area-associati/centro-studi/comunicazioni/item/11224-la-moda-maschile-italiana-nel-2019-2020).

Fig. 6.3 Monnalisa in pills: the main features emerging from the case. (Source: Authors' elaboration)

Marinella), respectively members of the third and fourth generation, manage the company.

The origins, however, date back to more than a century ago, when the founder decided to open a store in Naples. The company is, in fact, a historic company with more than 100 years of life. With the opening of a small store of about 20 square meters in 1914, the story of this extraordinary brand begins. Eugenio Marinella, the company's founder, decided to sell handcrafted and tailored products in the English style in those years. The company starts and then proposes its own style that will become unique worldwide from the English style tradition. English style is a synonym of elegance, which the company has been the bearer of since its origin. As mentioned, the company passes through four generations and more than 100 years of life and becomes one of the players with a globally known brand, which has its core business in producing ties. Elegance, refinement, tailoring, handmade are some of the features that characterize the product. A brand that has in its essence to be in Naples.

Naples is an area rich in sartorial traditions, and it is a widely recognized and famous city for its remarkable heritage all other the world. The link with Naples is one of the crucial aspects of the brand identity. Starting from Naples but remaining anchored to Naples is an essential aspect of the company.[8] Over time, while the tie remains the brand's core product, it has expanded its offers to include other product categories. It enlarged its proposal offering fashion items for men (such as knitwear, swimwear, or leather goods) and women (such as scarves and bags, or small leather goods). Although the company has a global reputation, it remains strongly rooted in the artisan dimension. In 2019 it reached a turnover of around 18 million euros.[9]

6.5.2 The Store in Naples and the Production Process

As stated above, the history of this company arises from the opening of a small store in Naples at the beginning of the last century. The store remains at the core of the company's business model. The Naples store is located in via Riviera Chiaia. It is the company's heart since it still represents one of the main assets for customer relationships. The store opens from 6.30 in the morning until the evening. It is a meeting place for customers who can experience the quality, exclusivity, elegance, and tailoring of the company's products. The company's business model is firmly anchored to the personal relationships with the customer and the sales method through the store is an excellent testimony of such relationships. The store is able to personalize the experience of the clientele buying the ties. Thus, the store becomes a destination for both customers and tourists who are visiting the city. They can also experiment with the typical hospitality of Naples. For example, the entrepreneur member of the third generation of the family points out that he usually has breakfast with the stores' first clients in the morning.

The company location at via Riviera Chiaia also hosts the production laboratory located above the store. The laboratory is another primary

---

[8] Considerations emerging from a company video accessible at https://www.youtube.com/watch?v=gAqnOw6HiGM

[9] https://www.pambianconews.com/2020/01/13/marinella-vuole-giovani-con-la-cravatta-283408/

asset of the company's business model. The company produces its ties meticulously by hand through the skilled work of a sartorial tradition. The entire production process is carried out in the laboratory. The raw materials used are of exclusive and precious quality. The company utilizes hand-printed silk made exclusively for it in England. Therefore, the laboratory produces handmade ties with a daily production that reaches 150 units, although the company receives requests from customers much above the daily production. The company's production offers unique styles and designs. There are roughly 1400 different patterns. Once again, this is an aspect that testifies the care and precision that the brand offers in its productions. The product is totally sartorial, as anticipated.

6.5.3 International Reputation, Presence in Foreign Markets, and Some Initiatives

The company, as mentioned, has achieved a global reputation, with E.Marinella becoming synonymous with elegant tie and sartorial quality all over the world. Over time, important personalities on a global level have chosen E.Marinella ties. It is not easy to list all the personalities who have worn an E.Marinella tie during its history, given that this list is long. It should include American Presidents (such as Kennedy and Bill Clinton), Presidents of the Italian Republic (such as Mattarella and Cossiga) rather than influential personalities of the business world (such as Gianni Agnelli and Aristotele Onassis), as well as members of royal families (such as Albert of Monaco and Charles of England). The list also includes prominent personalities from show-business, such as actors and directors. Other recognitions also testify the success achieved by the brand in terms of international visibility. In 2017 a selection of ties from the E.Marinella collection was exhibited at the MOMA (Museum of Modern Art) in New York. In particular, the ties were displayed in the exhibition section "Items: Is Fashion Modern?". Being included in the exhibition was an important recognition that clarifies E.Marinella's ability to represent an icon of ties production worldwide.

Interesting evidence emerges in terms of the brand's distribution presence. As anticipated, the Naples store represents the heart of the company. However, E.Marinella, over time, has managed to expand its presence, always remaining consistent with its profile. To date, distribution in the physical channel includes both E.Marinella single-brand and corners in important international stores. As for the single-brand stores, the company has other stores in the Italian market, respectively, in Milan and Rome. In addition, the company has opened two stores in Japan, the first of which was already established in 2007. In addition to single-brand stores, the company is also present with its corners in major foreign stores. It is present in European markets, such as France, Belgium, Spain, Switzerland, Germany, and non-EU countries, including the US, Mexico, and China, where it is present in Hong Kong and Shanghai.

In recent years, the company has also taken the path of e-commerce. This development path also was strengthened in response to the pandemic. Over time it has also expanded its distribution channels, offering part of its production to online multi-brand luxury retailers. In fact, since 2020, the company has been offering part of its collection in Mr. Porter's online e-store. This initiative also allows the company to expand its customer base in the youth segment.

In 2021, the collaboration between the E.Marinella brand and another Made in Italy brand, TBD Eyewear, aimed at creating a limited-edition capsule collection of eco-sustainable eyewear. This initiative highlights the company's ability to be innovative while remaining faithful to the values that have always characterized its offer.

E.Marinella is, therefore, a historical company of Neapolitan tailoring (see Fig. 6.4). Over the years, despite being smaller than other major luxury players, it has managed to achieve a solid global reputation. This reputation is the result of a sapient mix of values that the company still manages successfully. The ability to remain anchored to the values of the Made in Italy, with a particular emphasis on the sartorial tradition of Naples, is a fundamental aspect. The handmade production, the excellence of fabrics, and the product's elegance are other critical features of the business model. Then, the centrality of the relationship with the clientele remains crucial for delivering its value. The passion that the two

Fig. 6.4 E.Marinella in pills: the main features emerging from the case. (Source: Authors' elaboration)

generations of entrepreneurs now leading the company put into conducting the business is another central motive for the company's success. Finally, it should be noted that despite the success achieved in terms of global recognition, the company remains anchored to its sartorial and artisan origins, further evidence of the specificities of the business model.

References

Chakraborty, S., & Biswas, M. C. (2020). Impact of COVID-19 on the textile, apparel and fashion manufacturing industry supply chain: Case study on a ready-made garment manufacturing industry. *Journal of Supply Chain Management, Logistics and Procurement, 3*(2), 181–199.

Runfola, A., Milanesi, M., & Guercini, S. (2021). Rethinking interaction in social distancing times: Implications for business-to-business companies. *Journal of Business & Industrial Marketing, 36*(13), 105–115.

Sistema Moda Italia. (2020a). *La moda femminile italiana nel 2019–2020*. Available at: https://www.sistemamodaitalia.com/it/area-associati/centro-studi/comunicazioni/item/11265-la-moda-femminile-italiana-nel-2019-2020
Sistema Moda Italia. (2020b). *La moda junior 2019–2020*. Available at: https://www.sistemamodaitalia.com/it/area-associati/centro-studi/comunicazioni/item/11236-la-moda-junior-nel-2019-2020

7

Internationalization and Business Models of Luxury Fashion SMEs: Some Emerging Issues

7.1 Internationalization and Luxury Fashion SMEs: Why/How/What

In the two previous chapters, six cases of luxury fashion SMEs were presented with different characteristics but also common traits. The first two cases—Sapaf and Bontoni—are small businesses with a strong artisan vocation and a deep bond with the territory of origin. Both are located in industrial districts historically dedicated to the production of leather goods. In both cases, it is possible to speak of "genetic internationalization". In other words, the internationalization process started with the foundation of the company, it is an essential component not only of the business model, as already outlined by Guercini and Milanesi (2017) and Hennart et al. (2021), but of the company's DNA, so much so that we can speak of "*born global ante litteram*" companies, well before academic literature began to consider the phenomenon (Knight & Cavusgil, 2004).

The other four cases—Fabiana Filippi, Antonelli Firenze, Monnalisa, and E.Marinella—are medium-sized companies for which internationalization, often through major investments such as the opening of stores in foreign markets, has represented a driving force for the dimensional

A. Runfola et al., *Internationalization of Luxury Fashion Firms*, Palgrave Advances in Luxury, https://doi.org/10.1007/978-3-030-88755-1_7

growth and the skills developed. Even in these cases, internationalization has been approached by companies not as a simple development strategy but as a founding element naturally present in the very essence of the company. In other words, in all the cases presented, the companies did not pose the problem, at a more or less initial stage of their activities, whether it was appropriate or not to internationalize and in what ways. They have always experienced internationalization as a natural, genetic component of their business model, believing from the outset that their luxury products should find an outlet in international markets.

However, while the literature on luxury in general and luxury brand management takes the international projection of luxury companies for granted, the present study tries to outline some characteristics and dimensions of the internationalization of luxury fashion SMEs and the link with the business model. In the next sections, we analyze the elements that emerged in the three theoretical chapters (2, 3, and 4) of the book, summarized with the questions why/how/what, concerning the six cases: the motives for internationalization, how the process takes place, and the features of the business model of luxury fashion SMEs.

7.2 Why Do Luxury Fashion SMEs Internationalize?

What can be said about the reasons that push luxury fashion companies to internationalize? The six companies examined in the previous chapters certainly have a strong orientation to international markets that characterizes their evolution and business model. Chapter 2 presented and developed the hypothesis that luxury fashion companies have motives for internationalization deriving from the characteristics of the specific context in which they operate.

The companies presented in the previous chapters offer evidence of the internationalization process as a relevant element in the formation of the brand and company identity. For these SMEs, as well as for the large luxury fashion brands belonging to multinational groups, the global character of their notoriety and prestige is an essential condition of existence and development. So, let's go back to the motives for the internationalization of luxury fashion companies that have been presented and discussed in Chap. 2 (size of the demand, global image, customers' profile, management of distribution and communication channels) to see which of them have emerged from the cases studied and how.

Regarding the size of the demand, the companies analyzed find themselves in different situations. For Sapaf, the leather goods sector has always addressed a supranational demand. Business development cannot be separated from international growth. The business customers from distant countries have relied on companies such as Sapaf and others in its territory as suppliers. The market has, therefore, always been larger than the national one. The first exports started already in the year following the founding of the company and were directed to the American market, a primary foreign market in the history of the company. However, Sapaf has also benefited from the expansion in the Japanese market, which, for many years, has supported the international demand for the company's products. In the same way for Bontoni, the primary market has never been the national one, including from the beginning a broader area, mainly the American market. For this type of companies, it is not entirely correct to use the term export. In fact, the latter is usually associated with first national growth, followed by sales on foreign markets. In these two cases, the international projection characterizes companies right from the start. For both of these artisan companies, the skills and traditions are linked to a territory and a family, as the demand is genetically international.

In the case of Fabiana Filippi, the role of foreign markets is very important to allow the growth of the size of the potential demand. The company has experienced a period of growth that has led, in just over a decade, to almost fivefold its turnover. The company has achieved this result by offering its products in over forty markets. Internationalization is necessary to fuel the growth processes that in recent years have allowed the development of the company. As in the previous cases of Sapaf and Bontoni, the strong roots in the values and traditions of a small specific territory of origin are supporting elements to the brand image. For Fabiana Filippi, the motivation for internationalization seems to be a necessary choice to seek a development that would not be possible by selling exclusively in the country of origin. Quite similar considerations apply to the case of E.Marinella.

In the case of Antonelli Firenze, the international development, in addition to having similar traits to the previous cases, makes it possible to differentiate prices between different markets and to achieve overall greater margins in specific foreign markets rather than in the national market.

The search for international development is a key element for Monnalisa's growth, fundamental for the search for a different dimension of demand, not only quantitative (growth in volumes of potential demand), but also qualitative (acquisition of knowledge on international costumers due to the direct management of retail stores).

Regarding the customers' profiles, in the case of Sapaf, it can be noted that the global character of business customers leads to further geographical diversification of the exports. Thus, the company's first export is to Puerto Rico to satisfy the demands of a US department store. This type of situation is not just an anecdote but is emblematic of the global character of business customers, which, in the history of the company, have led to a diversification of export destination countries that is greater than the geographical diversification of customers. Although the company operates mainly in B2B markets, the final customer is defined as a "woman who belongs to a high-spending class, who can spend thousand euros for a bag", without highlighting boundary limits, as a transversal segment in all markets reached. In the case of Bontoni, the customer profile is studied by the management through the direct presence in the stores based in the most important foreign markets, starting from the main one, which is also in their case the US, followed by Europe and Russia. Considerable importance is given to the listening ability of the foreign customer, also in the case of Antonelli Firenze, and this indicates a form of growth in foreign markets that is not only made up of sales and direct investments but also of learning and progressive construction of knowledge. The characteristic of strong international mobility can also represent, to some extent, one of the motives for internationalization for other companies with a network of retail stores at an international level, such as Fabiana Filippi and Monnalisa.

As for the global image, Sapaf enjoys an international reputation in B2B markets; the company is also satisfactorily pursuing a progressive growth of a digital store for its brand, in which the target customers are largely international. For Bontoni, too, notoriety is widespread among a group of buyers and professionals. In the case of Bontoni, the main mechanism for building a global image in B2C markets is given by word of mouth, finding in this mechanism a fundamental factor for the development of the company's reputation internationally. In the construction of a global image by Bontoni, a role is certainly played by the network of stores where the product is sold, as in the case of Fabiana Filippi.

In all the cases analyzed, the presence of a growing number of foreign markets is linked with a strong identification with the values of a local territory in the region of origin. The image sought by each company is, therefore, not an image of a strong international company, but rather of a company that is rooted in local traditions, whose global image benefits from its ability to identify with a local community. In companies like Antonelli Firenze, in fact, the identification with a local territory, the creation of a rigorous Made in Italy, and the relationship with a local community become a basis for building an image that also supports the company's internationalization process. The growth of the company, therefore, seems more supported by an image linked to a specific origin, local territories, and traditions, rather than by a global image. It is the link with the local context (such as Antonelli Firenze's "Made in Tuscany") that supports the development of the company also on the international front, instead of, vice versa, the search for a global image that supports the local context of origin.

In the case of E.Marinella, which has achieved exceptional results in terms of the international reputation of the brand, internationalization seems to be the consequence of an image based on a strong connection with an important local context (the city of Naples). In other words, the companies under study find a basis for their international development in an image strongly characterized by a specific local context. In this sense, all the cases examined testify the strong links with the local context to which they belong, presenting this as a key element of international development.

Finally, regarding the characteristics of the communication and distribution channels, there are some differences in the cases. For instance, in the case of Sapaf, the role of participation in trade fairs and events dedicated to customers is particularly relevant, often organized in a context of collaboration with other companies in the sector, frequently from the same area of origin of the company and with similar characteristics. The issue of the role of the characteristics of distribution channels emerges as important both in the case of Monnalisa and in that of Fabiana Filippi. For both companies, retail stores in international markets become a key element of the internationalization and learning process, often directly involving the company management. Additionally, communication in all the cases concerns some key dimensions: the use of digital media, especially social networks (mainly Instagram) to communicate with an international clientele, the participation in fashion events, the role of word of mouth, and personal relationships with relevant customers.

7.3 How Do Luxury Fashion SMEs Set the Internationalization Process?

As highlighted in the introduction, the internationalization process of luxury fashion SMEs starts with the foundation of the company, being a genetic component of it and a fundamental part of its business model. An emblematic example that perfectly summarizes this statement is the case of Sapaf, in which the first invoice to Puerto Rico was issued in the early 1950s, only a year after the company was founded. Regarding the dimensions of the internationalization process, the four aspects previously discussed in Chap. 3 are examined below: the supply chain management and sourcing strategies, entry modes, the role of digitalization and e-commerce, and the liabilities in internationalization.

The sourcing and supply chains are mainly in the country of origin. Indeed, the companies analyzed operate in local systems, such as industrial districts, where suppliers are also located and with whom, in all cases, stable and lasting relationships have been developed over time (Guercini & Milanesi, 2019), based on trust and exchanges of ideas and know-how.

To name a few, Bontoni is located in the footwear district of Montegranaro, Antonelli Firenze buys fabrics in the historic textile district of Prato, Sapaf is located in the leather goods district of Scandicci and organizes collective actions with other companies in the district through a consortium. Local systems are carriers of knowledge, skills, know-how, which represent a source of enrichment and growth for the companies that are part of it and allow the development of B2B relationships that are consolidated over time.

It is necessary to highlight the manufacturing nature of the companies analyzed. Firmly supervising some—or all—phases of the production process (Brun et al., 2008), often still with marked characteristics of craftsmanship (Caniato et al., 2011), is a source of competitive advantage and guarantees companies unique know-how, as well as an important capacity for product and process innovation. In all cases, the critical and high-value phases of the production process (such as design and cutting) are always carried out directly by the company, while some phases can be outsourced, albeit within the boundaries of local systems. This is closely linked to two dimensions relevant to luxury fashion SMEs: the country of origin and flexibility. The role of the country of origin is fundamental for luxury since Italy is globally recognized for the excellence of "Made in" luxury. At the same time, the presence of a local supply chain made up of well-established relationships makes it possible to deal with fluctuations in demand with dynamism and flexibility. Both of these elements are at the basis of the possibility of effectively addressing the internationalization process, in which, therefore, the Made in Italy is enhanced, and companies leverage on local and efficient supply chains, which guarantee very high-quality standards. Finally, the maintenance of supply relationships at the local level is part of the will to pursue social sustainability linked to the maintenance of employment levels in the local systems and boost their growth.

About the entry modes into foreign markets, the six cases presented have different behaviors in part. Although in all cases the internationalization process starts from the beginning, how this happens can be different. In some cases, such as Sapaf or Antonelli Firenze, internationalization takes place through exports often supported by a consolidated network of agents. It is an entry mode that involves fewer risks and investments but has ensured, over the years, widespread penetration of foreign markets, even those that are geographically more distant.

In other cases, the main way to enter foreign markets, in addition to e-commerce, which we will discuss later, is the opening of retail stores. In this, it is possible to affirm that the behavior of luxury fashion SMEs can be comparable to that of large luxury fashion companies, which, for years, have been investing in the creation of an international network of stores (Moore & Burt, 2007; Moore et al., 2010; Guercini & Runfola, 2016). While Bontoni and E.Marinella are in an initial phase of experimentation in the process of opening stores, Fabiana Filippi and Monnalisa have always considered this entry mode as a priority, making it the fulcrum of their international marketing strategy. The opening of stores can have different characteristics in terms of store management. In particular, a distinction is made between directly operated stores, directly controlled and managed by the company with its staff, and third-party operated stores opened through agreements with local partners. The latter can be adopted in those foreign markets that are geographically and/or culturally distant, for which the presence of a local partner becomes fundamental for the success of the investment, as already highlighted by Milanesi (2020). The role of department stores and multi-brand stores is also relevant, as in the case of Antonelli Firenze, even if multi-brand stores have been severely impacted by the outbreak of the pandemic.

As regards digitalization and e-commerce, all cases are representative of companies that have heavily invested both in the digitalization of the company, in terms of management of production, organizational processes, and relations with B2B and B2C customers, and on e-commerce, through the development of a digital store, except for the case of Bontoni. The digital store, if present, is immediately designed for an international clientele: this is evidenced primarily by the languages into which the website is translated and the countries in which products are shipped.

In addition to investing in the digital store, in some cases—such as Antonelli Firenze and Monnalisa—the products are also sold on websites of online multi-brand retailers, such as Yoox or Farfetch. Selling through online multi-brand retailers may not weigh much in terms of volumes, but it certainly represents a strategic choice aimed at guaranteeing international visibility to the brand, as many of the online multi-brand retailers are global players. In other words, it involves adding a distribution channel that allows you to reach a global clientele with strength, even in those markets not covered by the company or where the product is not shipped.

Furthermore, in all cases, digital marketing tools are used strategically and as a means of communication aimed at a global clientele. In particular, the use of social media is emphasized, primarily Instagram. More generally, digitalization and e-commerce are designed to increase the integration of physical and digital channels. The drive toward showrooming by Monnalisa is a prime example. The goal is, therefore, an omnichannel approach (Ozuem & Azemi, 2017; Silva et al., 2020) with particular emphasis on the integration between physical and digital stores.

Finally, the issue of liabilities deserves further attention. The apparent liability of smallness, connected to the size of the company, does not seem to act in the cases of the luxury fashion SMEs examined, some of which have also undertaken paths of dimensional growth up to medium size. Nevertheless, even before the growth in size, the character of smallness did not prevent the start of a process of internationalization. Moreover, the cases are emblematic of a business model based on “Made in”, high product quality, and orientation to international markets, which is typical of the fashion/luxury sector, not only in Italy. The international development of the six luxury fashion SMEs is also linked to the growth of the upper class in the era of globalization. Thus, distance in its different forms—cultural, psychic, and geographical—is seen more as a resource that allows enhancing the offer with a particular national origin or “Made in”. In the cases, the liability of foreignness does not consist of additional costs (except for logistics costs, customs costs, and possible disadvantageous exchange rates, all costs that in any case concern the internationalization process of any company) or discriminatory treatments. Instead, it is possible to underline an advantage of foreignness (Brannen, 2004) related to the value of the country of origin. In other words, the specific country of origin, Italy, in a specific context, that of luxury fashion, in which Italy is one of the leading countries, mitigates the liability of foreignness into an asset and put the Italian luxury fashion SMEs in a position of competitive advantage in foreign markets. Moreover, the problem of distance, be it cultural, geographical, or psychic, does not seem to impact the market selection since, in all cases, the companies select even geographically and culturally distant markets for their attractiveness and business opportunities from the beginning of their internationalization process, despite the perceived distance and possible associated risk. This is even more evident in the opening of stores in foreign markets. Even when the companies rely on partnerships with local actors, they still have a high degree of control over the stores, thus generating processes of learning and gaining experience. In other words, the opening of a store, more than other entry modes, seems to be a way to get a position of insidership in the foreign market and gain the knowledge and capabilities to continue the international expansion. The real problem of luxury fashion SMEs can be the liability of localness. Luxury calls for internationalization, and not being international may represent a source of liability. Luxury is characterized by a series of features linked to the consumer profile, the need for a global image, the dimension of demand, the role of communication and distribution. Localness involves a lack of international genetics and, therefore, the failure to achieve an international dimension that allows an effective and efficient competition in the luxury market. Localness may be a source of competitive disadvantage compared to other luxury SMEs that are genetically international. The lack of a global image, a demand in the country of origin too narrow to support the company's development, the inability to reach consumers with specific profiles in international markets, and the lack of advantages related to the management of communication and distribution channel at a global or at least international level, may originate a liability of localness for luxury SMEs.

7.4 What Are the Implications of Internationalization for Business Models of Luxury Fashion SMEs?

In this section, we intend to answer the question: what are the implications of developing internationally for the business model of SMEs? Being international in the luxury industry implies that the international dimension should be related to each business model component. This section proposes some reflections emerging from the empirical investigation. One must remind that in Chaps. 5 and 6, we analyzed the cases of business models attributable to companies from the Italian luxury fashion industry. All offer brands for the final market. Only in the case of Sapaf, the company that still operates as a supplier of luxury companies in parallel with its consumer brand. Each case is unique and proposes a firm-specific business model. However, we try to offer some lessons learned from cases about the interplay between internationalization and business models. So, how does internationalization shape the business model of SMEs?

From our analysis, the international dimension of the business model can be traced back to some pillars. These pillars are the following:

(a) The international orientation of entrepreneurs is a strategic asset, implying that *entrepreneurs' international orientation is a fundamental resource underlying the model.*
(b) Value proposition leverages country of origin and refinement so that *international luxury brands proposing a country of origin and refined concept of quality.*
(c) Manufacturing is a critical asset for foreign development, so that *manufacturing skills are at the company's core and enablers of foreign development.*
(d) Relationships with international customers are a driver for development, so *interpersonal relationships are a resource for international expansion.*
(e) Retail and omnichannel orientation integrates the wholesale channels in the sense that *wholesale channel as a primary channel while retailing as a developing strategy for delivering value abroad.*
(f) New technologies and digital channels support foreign growth; hence, *investments in technologies and digital marketing tools for internationalization amplify the company's luxury brand awareness.*
(g) Regarding the costs of the business model, the economic and financial sustainability of international growth is a critical driver; hence, *international development follows an economically and financially sustainable growth model.*

Entrepreneurs' International Is a Fundamental Resource Underlying the Model. The first international dimension of the business model concerns the entrepreneur's international orientation. The potential in international terms of the business model depends on the entrepreneur's ability to conceive a company with an international positioning. The international mindset is then fundamental. Since its inception, the company, despite being in a local context, assumes an international vocation. This international vocation mostly translates in significant sales abroad, with foreign markets being the primary market since the beginning. This aspect is valid for almost all the companies investigated in the previous chapters. The case Bontoni represents an example. It is an artisan company that destines all production only to foreign markets since its inception. However, the international vocation also refers to reaching a global positioning in the luxury market. The case of E.Marinella is representative of this aspect. It became a global icon for ties production, although strictly anchored to the store in Naples. In general, it is the entrepreneur who guides the business vision of luxury. The entrepreneur defines the founding characteristics that make the company emerge in the world of luxury. In all the six cases analyzed, the entrepreneur is part of a family leading the company. This aspect strengthens the need for all family members to pursue internationalization. The entrepreneur or the family who leads the company remain strongly present in all business processes abroad. Thus, this kind of entrepreneurial companies take a lever on the entrepreneur's presence in its activities. In creating the luxury brand, the personal conviction of the entrepreneur to destine the offerings to international markets is then fundamental. For example, the entrepreneur is essential for managing relationships with international luxury customers (final consumers and intermediaries). Despite some differences between small-sized artisan companie and the medium ones, a vital resource of the business model is the entrepreneur's openness to internationalization in all six cases.

International Luxury Brands Proposing a Country of Origin and Refined Concept of Quality. Establishing a brand internationally in the world of luxury is challenging, especially for small- and medium-sized players. Difficulties can be approaching different foreign markets and competing with prominent players with higher resources and financial capabilities. In this context, the business model can rely on a luxury concept that proposes an alternative and different story based on quality. It is a country of origin story of luxury quality. It makes it easier to establish a dialogue with foreign partners and international consumers. In this sense, in the cases analyzed, the dimension linked to heritage, the manufacturing traditions of luxury, and the history of the people who founded the company emerges strongly. For example, the case of Fabiana Filippi. The company thrived within the international luxury industry by leveraging quality, craftsmanship, and sustainable issues starting from the region's heritage. Hence, the company can tell foreign markets a fascinating Italian story of quality.

In general, the country of origin is part of the values transmitted. Hence, quality is crucial in the value proposition and it is at the core of the luxury offering. Again, we can remind the cases of Sapaf or E.Marinella, which are strictly anchored to the luxury local traditions respectively of the Florentine leather industry and the sartorial heritage of Naples. Quality is associated with the stylistic content of the brands. Beyond the differences between companies, the possibility seems to emerge for SMEs to break into foreign markets through the proposal of non-ostentatious quality luxury. In this sense, the business model can lead the company to become a leader in a global niche or, in any case, to propose iconic products for specific international market targets. It, therefore, seems that international branding strategies are more oriented to explain the quality of the product than to affirm the "logo". Therefore, the logo is important, as much as the possibility of developing an awareness of the product's characteristics. What is behind the product is as well as necessary. In the international arena, customers should recognize the product for the quality and then for the logo.

Manufacturing Skills Are at the Company's Core and Enablers of Foreign Development. Another dimension of the business model concerns the role of manufacturing for international expansion. A fundamental dimension concerns the management of manufacturing and production skills. Companies manage manufacturing at a local or national level. They keep it as an essential asset of the company. Manufacturing is considered crucial for being international. Coming back to the etymology of the word, manufacturing comes from the Latin expression "*manu facĕre*",[1] which means made (*facĕre*) by hands (*manu*). In almost our cases,

[1] https://www.treccani.it/vocabolario/manifattura/

it seems that manufacturing activities remain at the company's core. Hence, the investment in manufacturing and training to maintain these skills at a local level is primary for the internationalization of the business model. It, therefore, seems to emerge that manufacturing is the basis for internationalization as it enables international development and drives the process. Hence, the manufacturing must remain internal or at least strongly characterizing the skills of the company. So what is the relationship between the business model and internationalization concerning production? It is the maintenance of the production dimension that drives foreign development.

Consequently, other investments and international strategies, such as a direct presence in foreign retail activities, always remain anchored to the need to maintain the manufacturing vocation and know-how. The business model feeds on an organization that maintains its highly productive nature. The production and its control allow telling unique stories of the country of origin. At the same time, they are at the basis of the quality of the product. Of course, production relates to traditions of local contexts in our empirical investigation. The origin of the product is a fundamental asset, so that foreign development should not contrast it. Hence, it is the production that guides international expansion, not the opposite.

Interpersonal Relationships Are a Resource for International Expansion. One of the main assets in the international development of the business model concerns the company's ability to establish relationships with foreign consumers and intermediaries. It allows, in many cases, to connect with international targets not only through the traditional communication and distribution channels of the luxury business. Instead, such an ability allows the possibility of having personal relationships with customers. Through these relationships, companies can explain how (and where) the product is produced and the people behind the company. Interpersonal relationships in foreign markets are managed directly by entrepreneurs and company staff (especially in those having a larger dimension). In luxury artisan companies, the entrepreneur also personally manages the relationships with consumers in-stores. For example, in Bontoni, the owner personally gets in touch with foreign clients, frequently spending short periods abroad and being present in the trunk shows. However, even in larger companies, in which, although there is a more structured commercial organization, the role of personal relationships with customers is one of the critical assets. The relationship with the customer, combined with the product's characteristics, favors international word-of-mouth processes that drive the expansion of the business model abroad. The customer is fundamental to spread the characteristics of the fashion luxury brand abroad. SMEs may not access luxury communication strategies at an international level. Hence, international word of mouth enables a growing brand awareness in the luxury industry.

Wholesale Channel as a Primary Channel While Retailing as a Developing Strategy for Delivering Value Abroad. The business model is internationally successful if it delivers the value proposition. Concerning this, in the empirical investigation, wholesale plays an important role. From this perspective, the incremental growth in terms of distribution investments is evident, especially when comparing cases with smaller dimensions with larger companies. Retail investments have a weight, especially in larger companies such as Monnalisa and Fabiana Filippi. Once again, the retail dimension is part of a growth logic that characterizes international luxury. However, the strong manufacturing vocation of companies remains prevalent compared to the retail dimension. Therefore, the manufacturing soul of the business still seems to constrain the distribution choices. It does not mean that physical distribution and online channels are not essential. Instead, companies implement an omnichannel logic. Nevertheless, the international business model primarily delivers value through indirect channels by resorting to prestigious retail stores abroad.

Investments in Technologies and Digital Marketing Tools for Internationalization Amplify the Company's Luxury Brand Awareness. The relationship between technologies/digital tools and the internationalization of the business model also follows specific logic. The need to be international nowadays requires digital marketing tools and new technologies emerging from the Industry 4.0 industrial paradigm. One may consider technologies and digital paths necessary even for SMEs. The COVID-19 pandemic has strengthened this need for every company, including luxury brands. The smaller and larger companies in our empirical investigation have developed technological solutions in production and/or marketing digital tools. Sapaf is an exemplificative case in our investigation. Although its small size, it is a pioneer player regarding investment in technologies and digital tools among leather manufacturers. The double soul (supplier and fashion brand) lets the company leverage its technological skills in B2B and B2C markets. However, we argue that digital tools help support a brand vocation that requires consistency with managing manufacturing, quality, and a specific relationship with the market targets. Take, for example, the case of Fabiana Filippi and recent investments in Industry 4.0, which aim to support the craftsmanship dimension.

The digital channel seems not to become prevailing for delivering value in foreign markets. Therefore, the business model leverages both the development of e-commerce channels and the use of selected international online multi-brand platforms. However, companies manage the digital channel to amplify brand awareness. In addition, new technologies and digital marketing tools support the manufacturing vocation.

International Development Follows an Economically and Financially Sustainable Growth Model. International development is always a risky but almost costly strategy to implement. It is well known that foreign growth requires financial resources and is naturally subject to risks. Hence, the cost dimension that supports the development of luxury brands abroad is particularly challenging, especially for SMEs. Hence, another essential feature emerging from our empirical investigation regards proposing an international dimension of the model considering the need to maintain its economic and financial sustainability. What is evident from the cases is the ability to develop in foreign markets consistently with a planned approach that profoundly reflects the economic and financial consequences of the choices made. So, if the international dimension of the model is considered one of the essential aspects, the choice is made in a highly reasoned and weighted way. We may remind the case of Antonelli Firenze and the company's strong attention to EBITDA and turnover, as described in Chap. 6. To generalize, the ability to start internationally and gradually increase international sales (and international markets) is then fundamental. Thus, an approach that avoids "biting off more than one can chew" seems to emerge. The international dimension of the business model is a step-by-step process. In essence, one of the main components of the success of the luxury business models described from an international standpoint regards the ability to reconcile foreign development with economically and financially sustainable company growth. To summarize, the international dimension shapes the business model in almost all the components. Moreover, the described dimensions seem to emerge as recurring features.

7.5 The Business Model of Luxury Fashion SMEs

This paragraph summarizes the characteristics of the business model of luxury fashion SMEs. The reflections emerge from the answers to the previous why, how, and what questions. These characteristics are transversal and typical of the business models of small- and medium-sized luxury companies, beyond their genesis (thus including both B2C companies and vertically integrated suppliers). In this paragraph, we propose the specificities of the model, the differences, and the similarities concerning luxury MNEs and SMEs (non-luxury). Finally, we outline the components of the business model of luxury fashion SMEs and how internationalization helps define them. Figure 7.1 below shows the main characteristics of the model, focusing on how companies create value (*value creation*), transmit value (*value delivery*), and capture value (*value capture*) in international markets.[2]

Concerning *value creation*, the business model of SMEs has a series of fundamental traits that contribute to defining the luxury proposal of these companies. The first is the international mindset. For these companies it means not being linked to the context of origin as the first or primary target market. As in the case of luxury MNEs, luxury SMEs are

[2] Figure 7.1 shows an elaboration of the components of the business model of luxury fashion SMEs based on the definition of business model proposed by Teece (2010) who indicates the value creation, value delivery and value capture mechanisms (see Chap. 4, Sect. 4.1).

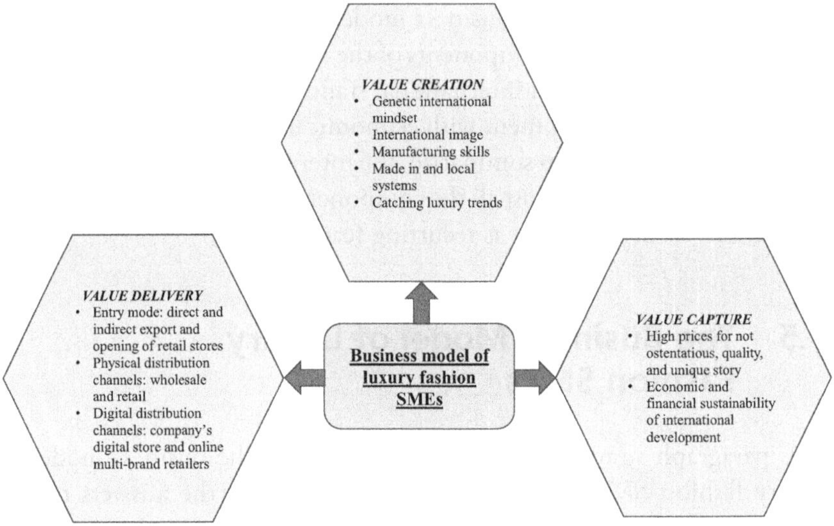

Fig. 7.1 The business model of luxury fashion SMEs. (Source: Authors' elaboration)

genetically international. For luxury fashion SMEs, the international mindset relates to the firm's entrepreneurial orientation rather than its multinationality. However, it is a different element than non-luxury SMEs since these companies are usually associated, especially in the management literature, with growth that starts and develops from the national market. In fact, except for born globals, SMEs are not usually considered international players from the inception. Luxury fashion SMEs tend to be genetically international, identifying the natural outlet for their products in international markets from the beginning. Due to this, they develop an international image of the company. The second dimension of value creation concerns manufacturing skills. These skills characterize the offer of the companies, as already highlighted. The most strategic phases of the production process are internal, or the company carries out the entire process. Compared to large MNEs, luxury fashion SMEs strongly preside over manufacturing within the company boundaries. It does not mean that they do not invest in distribution activities, but manufacturing is considered a key asset for success in international markets. The investments made in distribution activities lead to a strategic mix of skills ranging from manufacturing to retailing and configuring companies as vertically integrated. A third aspect concerns the link of manufacturing skills to local production contexts. In this sense, the "Made in" and local systems of luxury fashion companies represent elements through which SMEs create value. Even large MNEs can—and usually do—rely on local productions and contexts that are the result of manufacturing traditions. However, compared to large MNEs, luxury fashion SMEs do not have the will to extend their production into global value chains. Instead, they remain in the local context, which represents a source of competitive advantage for them. Finally, like the luxury MNEs, the luxury fashion SMEs can capture the trends of the luxury business and reinterpret them consistently with their history and values. Therefore, the ability to read and interpret global trends is an aspect in common with large-scale luxury players.

As for *value delivery*, it is possible to propose considerations regarding entry modes in foreign markets and channels (offline and online) to make the value proposition accessible to international consumers. The entry modes used by luxury fashion SMEs include forms of indirect and direct export. Compared to large MNEs, therefore, more traditional entry modes are also used. These modes, such as indirect forms of export, are typically associated with SMEs. However, similarly to large MNEs and unlike non-fashion SMEs, entry into international markets recurs to the opening of retail stores abroad. As is well known, this is a mode that requires specific retail skills and high investments. It is interesting to highlight how the luxury fashion SMEs propose an omnichannel approach in terms of distribution channels. They manage both physical and digital channels. Concerning distribution channels, companies rely on wholesale and retail channels.

Similarly, companies propose their digital stores and also rely on online multi-brand international retailers. This distribution approach is something in common with the large MNEs and, to some extent, surprising. For SMEs, usually, the lower endowment of resources (financial and non-financial) could guide the company to select some of the alternatives. In the case of luxury fashion SMEs, the omnichannel approach tends to prevail. Compared to large luxury companies, omnichannel coverage in the various international markets tends to be less extensive. In terms of communication, luxury fashion SMEs rely heavily on activating word of mouth among customers and traditional luxury communication channels. Relations with the various players that make up the corporate network, including intermediaries and final consumers, play a crucial role. Finally, digital communication comprises digital marketing tools, such as social media and collaboration with influencers, like the large luxury fashion MNEs.

Finally, regarding *value capture*, the positioning of the SMEs proposal is consistent with the luxury segment. Luxury fashion SMEs manage to convince customers to pay high prices for a non-ostentatious, high-quality luxury product that offers a unique story. This trait allows companies to emerge and succeed in a world typically dominated by prominent luxury players. Furthermore, a characteristic feature of these companies is a strong focus on sustainable growth in terms of economic and financial development. Therefore, internationalization is not a choice for luxury fashion SMEs; they weigh each decision for its economic and financial repercussions. This attention makes the approach followed by these companies very similar to the managerial approach typical of luxury MNEs. However, luxury MNEs can leverage multiple managerial tools and organizational units/skills.

In summary, the characteristics of the business model in terms of value creation, value delivery, and value capture allow luxury fashion SMEs to overcome the liability of localness. Of course, this does not mean that the business model is free from difficulties or barriers in the internationalization process. However, the structuring of the components considering the international dimension enables these companies to be luxury players in a global arena. Moreover, each company, once the liability of localness has been overcome through specific strategies, can have a unique and different growth path in foreign markets.

References

Brannen, M. Y. (2004). When Mickey loses face: Recontextualization, semantic fit, and the semiotics of foreignness. *Academy of Management Review, 29*(4), 593–616.

Brun, A., Caniato, F., Caridi, M., Castelli, C., Miragliotta, G., Ronchi, S., … Spina, G. (2008). Logistics and supply chain management in luxury fashion retail: Empirical investigation of Italian firms. *International Journal of Production Economics, 114*(2), 554–570.

Caniato, F., Caridi, M., Castelli, C., & Golini, R. (2011). Supply chain management in the luxury industry: A first classification of companies and their strategies. *International Journal of Production Economics, 133*(2), 622–633.

Guercini, S., & Milanesi, M. (2017). Extreme luxury fashion: Business model and internationalization process. *International Marketing Review, 34*(3), 403–424.

Guercini, S., & Milanesi, M. (2019). Understanding changes within business networks: Evidences from the international expansion of fashion firms. *Journal of Business & Industrial Marketing, 34*(1), 192–204.

Guercini, S., & Runfola, A. (2016). How western marketers respond to the new middle class in emerging market cities: The case of Italian fashion marketers. *International Business Review, 25*(3), 691–702.

Hennart, J. F., Majocchi, A., & Hagen, B. (2021). What's so special about born globals, their entrepreneurs or their business model? *Journal of International Business Studies*, 1–30.

Knight, G., & Cavusgil, S. T. (2004). Innovation, organizational capabilities and the born-global firm. *Journal of International Business Studies, 35*(2), 124–141.

Milanesi, M. (2020). *Liabilities and networks in the internationalization of fashion retailing*. FrancoAngeli.

Moore, C., & Burt, S. (2007). Developing a research agenda for the internationalization of fashion retailing. In T. Hines & M. Bruce (Eds.), *Fashion marketing: Contemporary issues* (pp. 68–85). Elsevier Butterworth Heinemann.

Moore, C. M., Doherty, A. M., & Doyle, S. A. (2010). Flagship stores as a market entry method: The perspective of luxury fashion retailing. *European Journal of Marketing, 44*(1/2), 139–161.

Ozuem, W., & Azemi, Y. (Eds.). (2017). Digital marketing strategies for fashion and luxury brands. IGI Global.

Silva, S. C., Duarte, P., & Sundetova, A. (2020). Multichannel versus omnichannel: A price-segmented comparison from the fashion industry. *International Journal of Retail & Distribution Management, 48*(4), 417–4130.
Teece, D. J. (2010). Business models, business strategy and innovation. *Long Range Planning, 43*(2–3), 172–194.

8
Conclusions

The book dealt with the internationalization of luxury fashion SMEs. The three questions "why, how, and what" guided the book's path both in the theoretical and in the empirical chapters. Finally, the book explored internationalization and how it is linked to the business model of luxury fashion SMEs. In this final chapter, some summary elements are provided concerning the main theoretical and managerial implications emerging from the research.

From a theoretical point of view, the original contribution of the book concerns the analysis of luxury fashion SMEs, their internationalization process, and business model. Much of the international business and international marketing literature, in fact, focuses attention on the big luxury players, for whom the global dimension is almost taken for granted. However, the internationalization of luxury fashion SMEs deserves a more specific reflection since these companies are just as international as MNEs. This research has shown that internationalization is a characteristic feature of the business models of these companies as well (Guercini & Milanesi, 2017). The international development of luxury fashion SMEs allows deriving some significant theoretical implications,

A. Runfola et al., *Internationalization of Luxury Fashion Firms*, Palgrave Advances in Luxury, https://doi.org/10.1007/978-3-030-88755-1_8

which may be valid not only for the fashion industry but for luxury SMEs in a broader sense (Freeman et al., 2010).

First, this book has highlighted the genetic internationalization of luxury fashion SMEs. In many cases, luxury fashion SMEs are "*born global ante litteram*" companies. In other words, they generate most of their turnover abroad from the very beginning, and this is a phenomenon that appeared relevant well before the academic literature highlighted the emergence of this type of company. They are already born international. They do not become so. This does not mean that luxury fashion SMEs do not activate growth processes in foreign markets during their life. Rather, the moment of the foundation of the company is distinguished from the process of expansion abroad. International genetics means that, at the time of their foundation and the launch of their brand, companies already consider the global market as their target market.

Foreign markets approached first can be selected for various reasons. There may be initial opportunities in some markets, as well as serendipitous processes that bring companies into certain geographic markets rather than others, not necessarily because of a planned process (Meyer & Skak, 2002). After the launch of the brand, international expansion follows a path that leads companies to expand the range of foreign markets in which to operate. From this point of view, genetic internationalization turns into a more structured process of international growth. In this process, companies can find difficulties and liabilities due to their size and competition in luxury markets. However, luxury fashion SMEs do not question whether or not to continue internationalization but instead pursue it in the belief that only through internationalization they manage to be successful.

Second, the book proposes the concept of *liability of localness*. The previous chapters have highlighted that liabilities for luxury fashion SMEs are not linked to development in foreign markets in the sense of a barrier to becoming international. Rather, not being international in luxury represents a source for liability. Luxury is characterized by a series of features linked to the consumer profile, the need for a global image, the dimension of demand, and the management of communication and distribution channels. Localness involves a lack of international genetics and, therefore, the failure to achieve an international dimension that allows an effective and efficient competition in the luxury market. Although internationalization is a challenging process, not taking this path from the beginning puts luxury SMEs in an unfavorable competitive position.

Therefore, the liability of localness leads to a lower performance for luxury SMEs that are not international. In essence, the theoretical debate has highlighted a series of liabilities for SMEs that include smallness, foreignness, and outsidership, the latter two specifically linked to internationalization processes (Johanson & Vahlne, 2009). This book adds another, which, however, proposes a different perspective from the previous ones. Internationalization for luxury companies can generate liabilities for SMEs in the process of both entry and growth in foreign markets, namely foreignness and outsidership, but also and above all in the formulation of the business model. The liability of localness requires the company to design the components of the business model, taking into account the international dimension. In other words, the business model has an international nature in order not to run into difficulties due to the liability of localness. Internationalization is, therefore, not just a strategy to be implemented but rather a dimension to consider in defining the components of the business model.

Finally, it is possible to discuss some managerial implications. The book examined successful cases of luxury fashion SMEs to derive best practices that are of interest both to luxury SMEs and to those interested in the world of luxury in general as managers, professionals, and scholars. So, what are the main implications for the management of luxury SMEs?

Luxury SMEs should avoid the liability of localness. Luxury calls for internationalization. Luxury SMEs should leverage a global demand and image, target defined profiles of consumers of luxury goods in international markets, and benefit from supranational management of distribution and communication channels. With these goals, entrepreneurs and managers should immediately consider internationalization not just as an option or a strategy to be pursued later, but as a part of the DNA, the essence of the company, and a transversal component of the business model. This does not mean that going abroad is not demanding and challenging. It means that internationalization is more a must than a choice, although it can be pursued in different ways. Rather, being limited to the domestic market means running into difficulties that can undermine the company's performance.

Furthermore, internationalization must be considered a genetic and transversal component of the business model. However, it must be taken into account that the international dimension must act differently on the various components of the business model. This means that not all the business model components must have an international character, which instead must have the mindset with which the model is designed. For example, it has been shown that an essential component of the business model concerns the production process, internalized or outsourced to suppliers located in the country of origin (often geographically close to the company), to exploit the "Made in" effect. This dimension of the business model supports the internationalization of the company but is not in itself international. In essence, being international does not mean that all components of the business model must be international.

Moreover, global trends matter for luxury SMEs, which must have constant attention to those trends that affect the luxury industry, such as sustainability and digitalization. These trends need to be captured. Luxury SMEs cannot fail to consider global luxury trends precisely because the arena in which they compete is the international or even global one. The sometimes very small size of luxury SMEs should not exempt them from grasping the trends of the luxury market on a par with large companies. Further examples of these trends are the growing weight of emerging markets and new generations of consumers, such as Generation Z, considered the new buyers of luxury products. In this sense, luxury SMEs must propose strategies and answers that can be specific and different from those of MNEs.

Finally, the international dimension of the business model must not make entrepreneurs and managers eager to go abroad at all costs or make risky investments. Internationalization as a characterizing feature of the business model, in other words, does not mean uncontrolled dimensional and international growth. The focus must be on the solidity, also at an economic and financial level, of the company. The approach to internationalization must always be careful, reasoned, calculated to balance growth in foreign markets with the company's economic and financial sustainability. In other words, entrepreneurs and managers must take into account an "incremental" approach to internationalization. The incremental nature of internationalization is not so much about the choice of markets, which can also be very distant geographically and/or culturally, nor does it concern the entry mode, which can also be complex and require investments, such as the opening of stores. The incremental approach must concern constant attention to the economic and financial solidity of the company aimed at pursuing balanced international, dimensional and qualitative growth. In this regard, international development may not always be linked to the dimensional growth of companies, which may remain small in size but still be relevant players in the global luxury market. The growth to be pursued can also be qualitative, related to relationships and capabilities.

Finally, entrepreneurs and managers should consider that the luxury business model is characteristic of each company, as each SME has highly specific and non-generalizable resources, skills, and know-how. Consequently, the business model should be declined differently according to one's identity. This involves two aspects. The first is that the benchmark with luxury MNEs may not always be a valid tool. MNEs have business models that, in some respects, are not comparable. Therefore, if some strategies can be pursued similarly, others deserve ad hoc policies for SMEs. Second, even the comparison with other luxury SMEs requires a reflection on the specific characteristics of one's business. Each company is different and has its business model, which must be appropriately designed.

In conclusion, this book started with a question: why write a book on the internationalization of luxury fashion companies? The relevance of luxury fashion SMEs in the global arena, with their specificities related to internationalization and the business model, represents an exhaustive answer. Besides large companies with globally known brands, the luxury industry includes other relevant players. The analysis carried out in this book has highlighted the existence of a variety of companies and has proposed themes, with both theoretical and managerial implications, which may be the subject of further academic and empirical research. However, the book is not intended to be a guide on how to manage luxury fashion SMEs successfully in international markets, the present work has attempted to turn on and shine the glittering lights of luxury on one of the industry's leading players: SMEs. These actors are very often behind the scenes of academic research and this book has tried to highlight their role and importance in the world of luxury. Let's go, luxury fashion SMEs, the international stage is also yours!

References

Freeman, S., Hutchings, K., Lazaris, M., & Zyngier, S. (2010). A model of rapid knowledge development: The smaller born-global firm. *International Business Review, 19*(1), 70–84.

Guercini, S., & Milanesi, M. (2017). Extreme luxury fashion: Business model and internationalization process. *International Marketing Review, 34*(3), 403–424.

Johanson, J., & Vahlne, J. E. (2009). The Uppsala internationalization process model revisited: From liability of foreignness to liability of outsidership. *Journal of International Business Studies, 40*(9), 1411–1431.

Meyer, K., & Skak, A. (2002). Networks, serendipity and SME entry into Eastern Europe. *European Management Journal, 20*(2), 179–188.

Index[1]

[1] Note: Page numbers followed by 'n' refer to notes.

A. Runfola et al., *Internationalization of Luxury Fashion Firms*, Palgrave Advances in Luxury, https://doi.org/10.1007/978-3-030-88755-1

The manufacturer's authorised representative in the EU is Springer
Nature Customer Service Centre GmbH, Europaplatz 3, 69115 Heidelberg,
Germany. If you have any concerns regarding our products, please
contact ProductSafety@springernature.com

Printed and bound by CPI Group (UK) Ltd, Croydon, CR0 4YY
30/09/2026
02225499-0002